CREATE! CONSTRUCT! QUEST!

THE GIANT BOOK OF

HACKS

FOR MINECRAFTERS

A GIANT UNOFFICIAL GUIDE FEATURING TIPS AND TRICKS OTHER GUIDES WON'T TEACH YOU

TOP SECRET

MEGAN MILLER

Sky Pony Press
New York

Sky Pony Press books may be purchased in bulk at special discounts for sales
promotion, corporate gifts, fund-raising, or educational purposes. Special
editions can also be created to specifications. For details, contact the Special
Sales Department, Sky Pony Press, 307 West 36th Street, 11th Floor, New York,
NY 10018 or info@skyhorsepublishing.com.

Sky Pony® is a registered trademark of Skyhorse Publishing, Inc.®, a Delaware
corporation.

Minecraft® is a registered trademark of Notch Development AB
The Minecraft game is copyright © Mojang AB.

www.skyponypress.com.

10 9 8 7 6 5 4 3 2 1

Manufactured in China, November 2017
This product conforms to CPSIA 2008

Library of Congress Cataloging-in-Publication Data is available on file.

Cover design by Brian Peterson

Print ISBN: 978-1-5107-2720-5
Ebook ISBN: 978-1-5107-2725-0

Printed in China

TABLE OF CONTENTS

Hacks for Minecrafters: Mods

COMMAND BLOCKS

HACKS FOR MINECRAFTERS

Welcome to the slightly crazy world of commands and command blocks. With commands, you can do all kinds of things that aren't possible in a regular Survival world. You can create a super-powerful zombie or a villager that will trade diamonds for dirt, build towers of emerald blocks, and instantly teleport to any location.

This book will show you how commands work, and it will look at the most popular commands for creating fun creatures and effects, whether playing by yourself or creating a map for others to play. You'll also see how you can use command blocks to create commands that anyone in your multiplayer world can use.

Because commands can very easily be typed incorrectly, I've created a text document (.txt) that contains the commands referenced in this book. You can download this text document from meganfmiller.com/commands. You can copy and paste the commands from the document into your own command blocks. However, you will need to check each command to see if there are any values you need to change so that the command works in your game and on your server. These are values like XYZ locations (where the command should occur) and player names. For creating your own custom commands, it can often be easiest to use an online command generator, and the addresses to several of these generators are included in this book.

There's no undo button in Minecraft.

Commands are very powerful, and some can change your world significantly. Remember that there's no undo button in Minecraft. As you are starting to use and understand commands and how they work, use a test world that you won't mind losing if disaster strikes. I've included instructions for creating a test world in the first chapter.

Lastly, some commands are a little different in varying versions of Minecraft. The commands in this book are created for Minecraft 1.9.

WHAT IS A COMMAND?

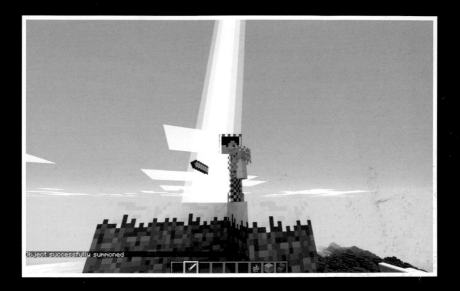

Object successfully summoned

A command, in Minecraft and many other computer programs, is a string of very specific words that the software is programmed to react to. Some commands in Minecraft give you items you wouldn't normally get playing a game in Survival mode, so these are sometimes called cheats.

For example, you can use the /xp command to give a player any amount of experience points (XP). That's pretty cheaty, but in a special mini-game, giving XP can be a great reward to players who have accomplished some specific feat.

There are commands for doing all different types of things in Minecraft. Some commands are used only by an operator, or op, for managing, allowing, and banning players on the server. These commands aren't available to use in command blocks. Other commands can only be used on players (like giving them XP) or on blocks (like putting a block at a specific location). There are also commands that affect the whole world, like changing it to nighttime or daytime. We'll look at these different types of commands (except for the server management commands) and how to use them in the following chapters.

NOTE: To use commands in a single-player world, you must either be playing in Creative mode or have created your world with cheats on. If you are playing on multiplayer, you must be a server administrator or operator (op).

You use commands in Minecraft in the chat window. For example, to give yourself 30 XP levels, you open the chat window by pressing T. Then type:

`/xp 30L`

You type in the chat window, at your screen's bottom left, to give a command.

This simple command gives whoever types it 30 full levels of XP, enough for the best enchantments!

Other commands are more complicated, and you must include ID numbers or names and codes that reference specific traits or other variables. For example, to create a tame black horse with white spots, a couple blocks away from you and wearing a saddle and diamond armor, you would type:

```
/summon EntityHorse ~ ~1 ~ {Type:0,Tame:1,
Variant:516,ArmorItem:{id:diamond_horse_
armor},SaddleItem:{id:saddle}}
```

To summon a tame horse with a specific color, markings, and armor takes a much longer command than granting someone XP.

The next chapter, Command Rules (or Syntax), will look at all the various parts of a command and how you put a command together.

Setting Up a New World

If you are playing and practicing with commands and command blocks, it can be helpful to set up a Superflat Creative world. The Superflat world is . . . super flat! There are no mountains, ravines, or rivers that can make it difficult to set up special areas or to concentrate on building.

To set up a new single-player Superflat Creative world to use for playing with command blocks:

1. Start Minecraft, or quit your current game, so that you are at the opening Minecraft screen. Choose Singleplayer to open up the Select World screen.

2. On the Select World screen, click Create New World.

3. In the Create New World screen, type in the name of your world (this could be something descriptive, like Command Block World). Click the Game Mode button until it says Game Mode Creative. Click More World Options.

4. In the World Options screen, click the World Type button until it reads "Superflat" and then click the Customize button that appears.

5. In the Superflat customization screen, click Presets to open the Select a Preset screen.

6. In the Select a Preset screen that opens, type the following into the top text box. (You may be able to correct the type that is already there, or just delete any existing text.)

```
3;minecraft:bedrock,52xminecraft:dirt,
minecraft:grass;1;
```

Select a Preset

Want to share your preset with someone? Use the below box!

3;minecraft:bedrock,52*minecraft:dirt,minecraft:grass;1;

Alternatively, here's some we made earlier!

- Classic Flat
- Tunnelers' Dream
- Water World
- Overworld
- Snowy Kingdom
- Bottomless Pit
- Desert
- Redstone Ready

Use Preset   Cancel

7. Click Use Preset. In the Customization screen that displays again, you should see that the layers for your world are 1 grass at the top, 52 dirt in the middle, and 1 bedrock at the bottom.

Superflat Customization

Layer Material	Height
Grass Block	Top - 1
Dirt	52
Bedrock	Bottom - 1

Remove Layer   Presets
Done   Cancel

8. Click Done to exit the Customization screen.
9. Click Done to exit the World Options screen.
10. Click Create New World to create your command block world.

CHAPTER 2

COMMAND RULES (OR SYNTAX)

For a command to work, you have to use only the proper words for that command, and these words must be in a specific order. These rules for how you type a command are called syntax. Each Minecraft command has a syntax that you must follow. (If you don't, the command may not work or may do something unexpected.)

Basically, you type the name of the command, followed by parameters. Parameters are words or numerical values that specify more about who, what, and where the command acts on. You may also hear these words referred to as *specifiers*.

The syntax for a command describes what words and parameters belong in the command and in what order they should be typed, along with the spaces and punctuation needed between words.

For example, the syntax for the /summon command is:

```
/summon <EntityName> [x][y][z] [dataTag]
```

This means that the summon command must start with a slash and the word summon. After one space (the spaces are important!) it must be followed by an entity name. You can also add coordinates in the XYZ format to indicate the location at which to create the entity. Finally, you can add additional data tags for more attributes of the entity.

You don't have to type in values for every parameter. The syntax is written in a way that makes it clear what you do have to type and what is optional:

Regular text = You must type anything in regular (not italic or slanting) text.

Italic text = Parameters you replace with your own values

<Angle brackets> = Parameters you must replace. Don't include the angle brackets.

[Square brackets] = Parameters you don't have to replace. Don't include the square brackets.

optionA|optionB = You must choose one out of the options shown.

IMPORTANT: Although you can omit parameters that are in square brackets, you must type in values for all parameters that are located before any used parameter. This is the only way the software knows what values belong to which parameter. In other words, once you omit a parameter, you can't include any parameters after this.

An Example Command

Look at this simple way to use the /summon command.

```
/summon Villager
```

The command begins with a slash (/). Any commands you type in a chat window have to start with a slash. If you're using a command block, you can leave the slash out, either way.

Notice there are only two words: the command name and one parameter—the required parameter, EntityName. Both of these are typed in regular text in the syntax, so you know they are necessary. But you don't type the parameter name EntityName. In the syntax, it was typed in italics, so you just replace the parameter with the actual value you want. (When you replace a parameter with the value you want, the value is often called the argument.) Here, you must type the official entity name that Minecraft assigned to the entity you want. This command is for a villager, so I used the villager's entity name, which is "Villager" with a capital V.

This simple command doesn't list any specific traits or career the villager should have, or where the villager should appear. So this command creates a random villager at the default location, which is wherever you (or a command block) are located in the world.

A More Complicated Example Command

A more complex version of the /summon command is:

```
/summon Villager 340 69 -220 {CustomName:
Fred,Profession:Profession:3,Career:3}
```

This command adds more parameters after the entity name Villager:

- **340 69 -220** These three numbers specify the XYZ coordinates to spawn the villager at. (And unless you're near that location, you won't see this villager being created!) Notice how these are typed with spaces in between. We'll go over how to use coordinates in commands and command blocks.

- **CustomName:Fred** This is a data tag that changes the name of the villager to Fred. The set of data tags starts with a curly bracket. The next chapter looks at how you use and format these data tags properly.

- **Profession:Profession:3,Career:3** This data tag says the villager's career should be Profession 3 (Blacksmith) and Career 3 (Tool Smith).

You can add a custom name to almost everything in Minecaft. This villager's custom name was added with the entity dataTag "CustomName".

Specifying Blocks, Entities, and Items

So if you have the syntax of a command, how do you know what values you can use for the parameters? What can you use for EntityName, besides Villager? We'll go over what your options are with each command we look at.

Pretty much each type of "thing" in Minecraft, from creepers to diamond ore to chests, falls into one of three main categories: blocks, items, and entities. Each object has a special ID name and/or ID number that you use in commands to specify that object. For each command, the explanations for the command syntax will tell you whether to use an ID name or an ID number. Most command syntaxes will call for an ID name, because Minecraft has been changing the code for commands to use the ID names rather than the numbers.

Almost all objects in Minecraft are categorized into three main categories: blocks (left), items (middle), and entities (right).

The appendices at the back of this book list many of these objects and their ID names and ID numbers. This means that when you look at a command syntax that asks for an <Item>, you can look in the Item ID appendix to find the ID for the item you want. When a command syntax asks you to use a Block ID, you can look in the Block ID appendix.

Spelling It Right

It's very important to type a command with no spelling, spacing, punctuation, capitalization, or other typing errors (typos).

If you don't, the command will either fail or give you unexpected results. For example, you could accidentally type in the wrong world coordinates to which to teleport a player. Wrong coordinates can lead to burning in a lava pool or suffocating inside an extreme hill!

When you enter a command into the Chat window, you will get a system notice saying whether it failed or succeeded. The exact message you get depends on the command you used, but a fail message will always be in red.

If you type a command incorrectly you will get a fail message. If you type it correctly, you will get a success message even if you use wrong information, like the wrong coordinates. So a success message doesn't always mean the command worked the way you wanted it to.

If your Minecraft chat window gets too busy with notices and announcements, you can clear it by pressing F3 and D.

When you are typing commands, try to think of each word not as a whole word but as a string of foreign characters. You have to look at every character, including spaces, to make sure it is the right one and is in the right order. One character missing is a fail, because programs like games aren't built to autocorrect spelling and punctuation.

Using Auto-Complete

The chat system's auto-complete can help you with typing some of your commands. You use the Tab key to have Minecraft show you what commands, or commands and specifiers, match what you've typed. (Auto-complete doesn't work if there is anything typed on the right side of the text cursor.)

- Type / and press Tab to cycle through available commands.

- Type / and the first few letters and then press Tab to see commands that match those letters.

- Type /, the command, and press Space. Now press Tab to see what parameters can follow the command.

If you type the slash and the first letter or letters of the command, and then press Tab, Chat will display the first possible command that has the same first letter(s). You can press Tab again to get more matches. After you type a command (and the space that comes after it), you can press Tab again to see what additional options there are, if any.

For example, to have Minecraft help you with the /gamemode command:

1. Type /g and press Tab. Continue pressing Tab until the chat window shows /gamemode.

2. Press the space bar to add a space.

3. Press Tab again to have Minecraft show the possible arguments for /gamemode. Stop when you see /gamemode creative.

4. Your command is complete, and now you can press Enter to execute it and switch to Creative mode.

You can press Tab when you are typing a command into the chat window to see suggestions in the notification area.

To have Minecraft help you with the name of a block or item, type "minecraft:" in the location of the command where you are inserting the block or item name. For example, type /give meganfairminecraft:m and press Tab to see all the items you can give that start with M.

For all the block and item ID names, you can add the word "minecraft:" (with a colon at the end and no spaces) in front of it. For example "minecraft:dirt" is the same as "dirt". Using "minecraft:" in the chat window allows the auto-complete function to help you with items.

Get Outside Help!

There are lots of command generators online that you can use to help you with your command. They have a form you fill out to select commands, parameters, and arguments. When you are finished, you usually click a button, and a text box will show you your finished command. Copy (Ctrl/Command+C) this text, go to Minecraft, and paste (Ctrl/Command+V) this copied command into the chat window or into a command block. With online generators, you do need to make sure that the generator works with your version of Minecraft.

Some online generators are:

http://www.minecraftupdates.com/commands

http://minecraft.tools

http://mcstacker.bimbimma.com

CHAPTER 3

CUSTOMIZING COMMANDS

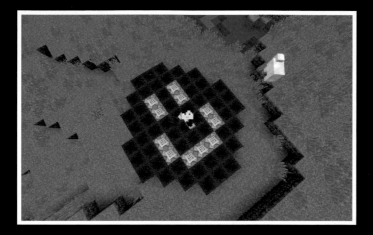

In Chapter 2, you saw how parameters are used with commands. Choosing values (or arguments) for some parameters is fairly simple, like choosing a Block Name. Others, like <X Y Z>, target selectors, and <dataTag>, are a bit more complex. There are a number of ways to use values for these.

XYZ Coordinates

The XYZ coordinates that you use in a command show the exact place in the world at which the command should take place or create something, along imaginary lines called axes. When you use XYZ coordinates, there's always an imaginary center at 0 0 0. In Minecraft, 0 0 0 is set to be around your original spawn point.

The Debug screen shows you the coordinates where you are standing, the block you are standing on, and the block you are looking at.

- **X:** Where you are on an east–west (X) line or axis. This number is negative when the location is west of the center.

- **Y:** Where you are on a vertical axis. This number is negative when the location is below the center.

- **Z:** Where you are on a north–south axis. This is negative when the location is north of the center.

The X-axis (red) shows where you are on an east–west imaginary line. The Y-axis (green) shows you where you are vertically. The Z-axis (blue) shows you where you are along a north–south line.

To find a coordinate, open up your debug screen by pressing F. Look for these entries in the bottom left section

- **XYZ:** This entry shows exactly where you are standing, with decimals.

- **Block:** This shows the XYZ coordinates for the block you are standing on.

- **Facing:** This shows which way you are looking.

- **Looking at:** This shows what block your cursor is pointing at. This entry only shows up when you are close enough to a block that it shows a thin line around it.

So when you need to enter a real XYZ coordinate for a command, you can go to the location you want it to appear. If you want it to appear above the block you are standing on or looking at, you'll have to add 1 for each block you are raising the location.

Relative Coordinates

You can also use relative locations. These say where the XYZ location should be in relation to where the command was given. This is either where you are when you enter the command in chat or where the command block is.

You specify an XYZ location with a tilde (~). The key for this squiggly line is usually at the top left of your keyboard. You use three tildes by themselves, in place of the XYZ coordinates, to set the location at the command-giver's location. You can also type a number, positive or negative, after any tilde to specify the distance in blocks, along that axis, away from the command-giver's location.

~ ~ ~: This makes command execute at the location of the command-giver.

~1 ~ ~-2: In this example, the X is ~1. This says the command must execute 1 block east (because it is a positive number) of the command-giver. The Y is the tilde by itself. So this says to execute the command at the same vertical (Y) position as the command-giver. Finally, the ~-2 for the Z position says that the command should execute 2 blocks north (because it is a negative number) of the command-giver's location.

Use the Debug screen (F3) to find coordinates for the block you are standing on and a block you are looking at.

Target Selectors

Some commands allow you to use target selectors. Target selectors let you select one or more players or entities without knowing their exact locations or names. You use a special target variable instead of a name or ID.

@p   This selects the nearest person to the command-giver.

@r   This selects a random player in the world.

@a   This selects all players in the world.

@e   This selects all entities in the world (including players).

You can also be more specific by using arguments with a target selector. Target selector arguments include:

x y z	Selects targets only at these XYZ coordinates (You can't use relative coordinates.)
r, rm	Selects targets only within the radius r from the XYZ coordinates. Rm selects targets only outside the radius.
c	Selects targets up to a certain amount (count)
m	Selects targets by gamemode. Doing [m=!*gamemode*] will select targets not on a certain game mode. A value of -1 will select all game modes.
l, lm	Selects targets with no more than a certain XP level. Lm selects targets with no less than a certain XP level.
name	Selects targets that match an entity name (either a player name or an entity that has been give a custom name)
type	Selects targets that match an entity type
dx dy dz	Selects targets within a large box. The box is dx wide, dz long, and dy high and has a corner at the location the command was executed
score_*name*	Selects targets with a scoreboard value in the objective "name" of no more than a certain amount
score_ name_min	Selects targets with a scoreboard value in the objective "name" of no less than a certain amount
team	Selects targets only on a certain team. Doing [team= !*teamname*] will select targets not on a certain team.
tag	Selects targets with a certain scoreboard tag. Doing [tag=!*tag*] will select targets without a certain tag.

When you use arguments for a target selector, you have to use argument:value pairs. These argument:value pair or pairs have to be enclosed in square brackets and typed without spaces. If there's more than one pair, you use a comma with no space to separate the pairs. Here are some examples of using a target selector, with the commands /xp and /tp (teleport):

/xp 2L @p Gives 2 XP levels to the nearest player to the command-giver

/xp 2L @p[x=-697,y=65,z=211] Gives 2 XP levels to the nearest player to the X Y Z location of -697 65 211.

/tp @a @r Teleports everyone to one random player's location

/tp @e [type=Creeper,c=4] @r Teleports up to 4 entities that match the type creeper to a random player. Very mean!

Working with Data Tags

Some advanced or complicated commands can have long strings of data tag parameters in them. These data tags help define the traits or properties of items, blocks, and entities. Data tags are grouped and enclosed in either square or curly brackets:

[List Tags]: Tags that are lists, or can have several values separated by commas, use square brackets. The square brackets let the computer software know that what follows is a list, and commas separate each different value.

{Compound Tags}: Tags that are defined as "compound tags" use curly brackets. A compound tag has an identifying parameter name, such as "id", followed by a colon ":", followed by a space and then the value "1". The curly brackets let the computer software know to expect this type of information and when it ends.

Data Tags and Data Values

Data tags are different from data values. Data tags are attribute: value pairs that describe various characteristics of an item or entity. Data values are additional ID numbers that specify a type of block or item. For example, the ID name for granite is stone, so its data value (DV)—which is 1—defines it as a granite block.

Here's an example of a very long command that gives the nearest player a chest with a couple of items in it:

```
/give @p chest 1 0 {BlockEntityTag: {Items:
[{id:stone,Slot: 0,Count: 23},{id:wool,Damage:
1,Slot: 1,Count: 12},{id:torch,Slot: 2,Count:
1},{id:diamond_sword, Slot: 3, Count: 1}]}}
```

Each item (starting with "id") is surrounded by curly brackets, and the list of items (after "Items") is enclosed by square brackets. Everything that the data tag "BlockEntityTag" refers to is also enclosed with curly brackets. Finally, all the dataTag parameters (everything after the "data" argument of 0) are enclosed in another pair of curly brackets.

The data values that you can use for different entities and items depend on that object. The Minecraft Wiki has a long list of what data tags (also called NBT tags) work with what item or entity, at http://minecraft.gamepedia.com/Chunk_format, under the heading NBT Structure.

Balancing Brackets

It is very important to make sure each opening bracket has a closing bracket to match it, at the right place. It is also incredibly easy to forget a bracket. Simple code editing software, like Atom for Mac or Notepad++ for Windows, can help highlight brackets that match or are missing. You can also use a regular text editor (TextEdit in Mac or Notepad in Windows) to write out long commands in a way that shows where the brackets are, so you can make sure they are balanced.

```
/give @p chest 1 0 {
    BlockEntityTag: {
        Items: [
            {
                id:stone,
                Slot: 0,
                Count: 23
            },
            {
                id:wool,
                Damage: 1,
                Slot: 1,
                Count: 12
            },
            {
                id:torch,
                Slot: 2,
                Count: 1
            },
            {
                id: diamond_sword,
                Slot: 3,
                Count: 1
            }
        ]
    }
}
```

In this notation, you put the brackets on separate lines, and indent pairs of brackets, so you can clearly see each pair of brackets and what they contain.

CHAPTER 4

USING COMMAND BLOCKS

ommand blocks are blocks that you place in the Minecraft world. Each command block can have one command assigned to it. To execute the command, you activate the block by sending it a redstone signal. The simplest way to do this is to place a button on the actual command block.

Differences between Command Blocks and Chat Commands

- Command blocks can take very long commands, while Chat entries are limited to 100 characters.

- Players without op status can execute commands in command blocks. (Only ops can place commands in command boxes, though.)

- Command blocks are much more powerful than Chat commands since you can control them with redstone.

- Two or more commands can be linked together by linking command blocks with redstone or using chain command blocks.

- Using relative coordinates in a command block means the location will be relative to the command block, not where you are.

Getting Command Blocks

Command blocks are very powerful, so they aren't available by crafting or in the Creative inventory. You have to use a command in the Chat window to get them. To give yourself a stack of 64 command blocks, type the following into the chat window:

```
/give @p minecraft:command_block 64
```

Adding Commands to Command Blocks

You must be in Creative mode to add commands to command blocks. To assign a command to a command block:

1. Place the block on the ground where you want it to be. Remember that its location will determine where any relative coordinates point to.

2. Right-click the command to open the command block interface.

3. Type (or paste) the command into the Console Command text box. (The box below is where the command block shows success or error messages for the last executed command. You can turn this off by clicking the button 0 to make it X.)

4. Click Done to assign the command and close the interface.

You type a command into the Console Command text box at the top of the command block interface.

Types of Command Blocks

There are three different kinds of command blocks. The default command block is orange and is called an Impulse command block. Impulse command blocks execute their commands only when they receive redstone signal.

If you place down an Impulse command block, you can change its type by right-clicking it to open the interface and clicking on the button that says "Impulse".

The other two types of command blocks are Repeat and Chain. Repeat command blocks will execute their command every tick (20 times a second!). This is useful if you want a command to always be running.

Be careful with what commands you put into Repeat command blocks! If you put a /give command, your inventory would quickly fill up!

Here's a fun command to try with Repeat command blocks. Grab a few snowballs and a few boats, and put this command into a repeat command block:

```
/execute @e[type=Snowball] ~ ~-4 ~ /fill ~-2
~ ~-2 ~2 ~ ~2 minecraft:water 0 replace air
```

Make sure to click the "Needs Redstone" button to change it to "Always Active". This command will make a pool of water below every snowball you throw! It can get out of hand pretty quick, but it's fun to ride around on the towers of water with a boat.

You might see your chat fill up with messages from command blocks. To turn this off, run:

```
/gamerulecommandBlockOutput false
```

WARNING: Using a Repeat command block to loop a command over and over again can use up too much memory and can crash your game or machine. When you are experimenting, use a test world that you don't mind losing if something goes wrong, or make a backup of your world.

The other type of command block is Chain. Chain command blocks are placed in a line, and when the first one in the line is activated, the next one activates, going down the line in order. This is useful for making chains or commands that need to be in order.

Activating and Linking Command Blocks

To activate an Impulse command block, you have to send it a redstone signal. While redstone is too big a topic to cover in this book, there are simple solutions for activating command blocks. You basically just need to attach a power source to the block and turn it on. For example:

1. Place a button or lever on the block. You will need to hold shift while right-clicking to do this. The lever has two positions, on and off, so you click it once to turn the signal on. Then, to repeat the command, you have to turn it off, and then back on again. The button automatically turns itself off, so each time you press it the block will execute the command. Make sure the command block is on Impulse, not Repeat!

2. Place a button or lever on another non-transparent block, and connect that block to the command block with redstone dust. The line of redstone dust must point directly at the command block.

Combining Command Blocks

You can connect command blocks in a line by setting the command blocks to Conditional. A Conditional command block will only run its command if the block behind it ran its command with no errors. They're a lot like Chain command blocks, except Chain command blocks don't check if a command failed or not, and you can use Repeat command blocks in the conditional chain as well.

You can also combine command blocks to the outside world with a redstone signal that links to each one, with redstone dust and/or redstone repeaters. A redstone repeater needs to face into the command block to send it a signal.

You can activate several command blocks at the same time by connecting them all to a single button, lever, or other power source.

TIP: It can be easy to forget what a command block does. Add a sign next to your command blocks that reminds you what each of them does.

BASIC COMMANDS

some commands are very simple, general commands. Some of these can be used by anyone, not just an op. Basic commands include:

/difficulty
/gamemode
/help
/list
/me
/say
/tell

The /difficulty Command

This command sets the difficulty level of the current game, which can be Peaceful, Easy, Normal, or Hard.

For example, you might use one command block to change your Normal Survival world to Peaceful, in order to kill all hostile mobs. When you are done playing in Peaceful, use a second command block to change the world back to Normal to set your game back to Survival mode. You can also connect these two command blocks with redstone, so that you first change to Peaceful to kill hostiles and then go immediately back to your Normal Survival mode.

Syntax

```
/difficulty <difficulty level>
```

- Replace <difficulty level> with one of the following:
  - peaceful (or p or 0)
  - easy (or e or 1)
  - normal (or n or 2)
  - hard (or h or 3)

Examples

```
/difficulty peaceful
/difficulty 1
/difficulty h
```

The /gamemode Command

This command changes a player's current gamemode to Survival, Creative, Adventure, or Spectator. (Hardcore isn't a true game mode—it combines Hard difficulty level with having only one life in a world.) This can be handy in a game map, where you want to change a player from Adventure mode to Spectator mode if they die (and are out of the game).

Syntax

```
/gamemode <mode> [player]
```

- Replace <mode> with one of the following:
  - ○ survival (or s or 0)
  - ○ creative (or c or 1)
  - ○ adventure (or a or 2)
  - ○ spectator (or sp or 3)

- May replace [player] with the username of a single player or a target selector. If you don't specify a player, you will change your own game mode. If you are using this in a command block, you must specify a player.

Examples

```
/gamemode s meganfair
/gamemode 0 notch
/gamemode c
/gamemode sp @p
```

The /help Command

Any player can use the /help command to get information about commands. You can type /help for a list of all commands (for pages beyond 1, also type the page number). You can also get help for a specific command by typing the command name after help.

Syntax

```
/help [page|commandname]
```

- Replace [page/commandname] with either a number from 1 to 7 for that page of help text or with the name of the command.

Examples

```
/help
/help 3
/help give
```

The /list Command

Any player can use the /list command, which simply lists all the players that are currently playing. You can also press the Tab key for the same information.

Syntax

```
/list
```

The /me Command

Any player can use this command to send a message to other players. This "me" message always begins with your user name.

Syntax

```
/me <any text>
```

- Replace <any text> with the text of your choice. You can include target selectors, like @p.

Example

```
/me makes sadface
```

This displays as: *meganfair makes sadface.

Notice that the message display starts with an asterisk (*) before your username. This lets other players know that the message is coming from another player.

If you are an op, you can also use target selectors in the <any text> you include. This will result in one or more targets' usernames being displayed. Also, if you use this in a command block, the message displayed will replace "/me" with "@". @ is the default name of the command block, but you can rename a command block with an anvil. Then the /me command will use the command block's given name. So, if you name a command block "The Flying Spaghetti Monster" and have it execute this command, it will show in Chat as:

*The Flying Spaghetti Monster makes sadface.

The /say Command

The /say command sends a message in the chat screen to all players. This is almost identical to a chat message, but you can use target selectors like @p to include usernames in the message. If a command block is programmed with the /say command, it will use "@" as its display name. You can rename the command block with an anvil to change the command block's name. A second difference from a chat message is that the sayer's name is enclosed in square brackets, rather than the angled brackets used for names in Chat. You can use this with command blocks to give general announcements or make it seem like a message is coming from someone else—whatever you name the command block.

Syntax

```
/say <any text>
```

- Replace <any text> with your message.

Examples

```
/say The server will shut down for
maintenance at 5pm EST
```

If I type this, the Chat will show:

[meganfair]The server will shut down for maintenance at 5pm EST

If a command block named "IMPORTANT" executes this, the Chat will show:

[IMPORTANT]The server will shut down for maintenance at 5pm EST

The /tell Command

Anyone can use the /tell command to send a private message to one or more players on the server. If an operator uses this command, he or she can use a target selector in place of usernames.

Syntax

`/tell <player> <any text>`

- Replace <player> with the username of the player you are sending the message to.
- Replace <any text> with your private message.

Example

`/tell BigRabbit Do you want to play Death Games?`

If I send this message to player BigRabbit on my server, BigRabbit (and only BigRabbit) will see the following message:

meganfair whispers to you: Do you want to play Death Games?

WORLD COMMANDS

World commands change something that affects the entire world or game. For example, the /weather command changes what the weather is, and the /time command changes what time it is in the game.

World commands include:

/defaultgamemode
/gamerule
/seed
/setworldspawn
/time
/toggledownfall
/weather
/worldborder

The /defaultgamemode Command

This command changes the game mode that new players on the server will be in: Survival, Creative, Adventure, or Spectator. You'd use this command on a multiplayer server, perhaps with an adventure map. You could use this command to make sure that every player that starts playing in the world is in Adventure mode, so that they can't break down buildings, for example.

In Spectator mode, you are invisible to other players. But if you press F5, you can see other players who are also in Spectator mode. You appear to each other as a transparent head floating around.

Syntax

`/defaultgamemode <mode>`

- Replace <mode> with one of the following arguments:
    o survival (or s or 0)
    o creative (or c or 1)
    o adventure (or a or 2)
    o spectator (or sp or 3)

Examples

`/defaultgamemode adventure`
`/defaultgamemode 3`
`/defaultgamemode c`

The /gamerule Command

The /gamerule command lets you set basic game options for your world or find out the current game options. You can also create a new game rule that you can use to store a value that you can retrieve and use later. This would be useful if you are combining command blocks to make a command block program.

Syntax

`/gamerule <rulename>[value]`

- Replace <rulename> with one of the game rules listed below.

- May replace [value] with a valid value for the game rule you are setting. This will generally be either true, false, or a number. If you don't type a value for the rule here, then the response will tell you what the game rule is currently set to.

Gamerules*		
GameRule	**Description**	**Values**
commandBlockOutput	If true, command blocks notify administrators when they execute a command. The default value is true.	true or false
doDaylightCycle	This stops and starts the sun and moon moving. The default value is true. You might use this on a map where you want it to be daylight the entire day, so that fewer mobs spawn naturally.	true or false

GameRule	Description	Values
doMobLoot	This allows mobs to drop items when they are killed, like zombies dropping rotten flesh. The default value is true. Turning this off means you also won't get meat from passive mobs, so you'll have to be a vegetarian, too.	true or false
doMobSpawning	This decides whether mobs (including passive and neutral mobs) should naturally spawn. The default value is true. Mobs can still spawn from spawners if this is set to false.	true or false
keepInventory	If you change this to true, whenever someone dies, all their inventory will remain with them. The default value is false. You might turn this on in a special Survival mini-game, where players die constantly. This allows them to get back into the fight quickly with their sword or bow and arrow.	true or false

GameRule	Description	Values
mobGriefing	This allows mobs to destroy or change blocks, such as creepers blowing up the landscape or sheep "eating" grass blocks and turning them into dirt. It also allows mobs like villagers, Endermen, and zombies to pick up items. The default value is true.	true or false
naturalRegeneration	This lets players naturally get back health points, as long as their hunger bar is high enough. The default value is true.	true or false
showDeathMessages	This turns on and off messages displaying in Chat when a player dies. The default value is true.	true or false

*This list is a shortened version of the full list on the Minecraft Wiki, which you can find at http://minecraft.gamepedia.com/Commands#gamemode

Use the mobGriefing option to turn off damage from creepers and other block-changing mobs.

Examples

```
/gamerule mobGriefing false
/gamerule NewGameRule 30
```

The second example shows how you can create and save a new game rule.

The /seed Command

The /seed command displays the number for the world seed. If you used regular words for your seed, such as "awesome new world", the seed is still displayed as a number. This is because when you type in letters for a seed, the letters are converted into numbers. The seed is what helps the Minecraft software create entirely different worlds with new terrain. If you know the seed for your world, you can share the number with someone else. He or she can play the same world using your seed (you do have to be using the same version of Minecraft). Knowing the seed number can also help you find things like slime chunks. There are several online slime chunk finders that will take your seed number and let you know what areas slimes will spawn in (besides swamps at night). One slime finder is at chunkbase.com. (A chunk is a 16x16x256 block section of the world, used in the game programming.)

The slime chunks in your world are based on your world seed number. Slime chunks are 16x16 areas where slime will spawn at any light level, and below y=40.

Syntax

```
/seed
```

There are no parameters or arguments for this command, just type /seed.

The /setworldspawn Command

The /setworldspawn command allows you to change the spawn location for your world. The spawn location is where new players appear and where you respawn when you die if you haven't slept in a bed somewhere. This can be helpful if the original world spawn is in an inhospitable area. If you've made a mini-game or adventure map, you may want players to start in a special location.

The /setworldspawn command lets you set the spawn for your world somewhere more convenient for you.

Syntax

```
/setworldspawn [x y z]
```

- May replace [x y z] with the coordinates you want. If you leave the command as /setworldspawn, then the location of the command block (or your location) will be set as spawn.

The /time Command

The /time command lets you change the time in your world to a specific time or to day or night. You can also use it to jump forward in time by a specific amount or find out how many ticks have gone by since midnight or the start of the world.

Time in Minecraft software is measured in ticks. There are 20 ticks in a second, so each tick lasts .05 of a second. Because a Minecraft full day/night cycle lasts 20 minutes in real time, this means there are a total of 24,000 ticks in a Minecraft day. From this, you can also determine that an in-game Minecraft hour lasts about 50 seconds in real time.

Syntax

```
/time set <add|query|set> <value>
```

- Replace <add|query|set> with one of the three options: add, query, or set.

- For "add", replace <value> with the number of ticks you want to add to the time, from 1 to 2147483647. To add a Minecraft hour, add 1000 ticks, and to add a day, add 24000.
- For "query", replace <value> with either "gametime" or "daytime". Gametime will return the total number of ticks since your world started, and daytime will return the number of ticks since midnight.
- For "set", replace <value> with either a number of ticks (from 0 to 2147483647), or day, or night. Setting the time to 1000 sets the time to day, and setting it to 13000 makes it nighttime.

Examples

```
/time set day
/time set 13000
/time add 24000
/time query gametime
```

The /toggledownfall Command

The /toggledownfall command is a simple command that lets you immediately start or stop downfall (rain or snow). If it is currently raining or snowing, the weather turns clear. If it is currently clear, it will start raining or snowing.

Syntax

`/toggledownfall`

There are no parameters for this command; you simply type /toggledownfall.

The /weather Command

You can use the /weather command to change the weather to clear, rain, or thunder. (If you are in a snowy biome, you'll get snow instead of rain. If you are in a desert biome, you won't see the rain, except at the borders to another biome.) The game will decide how long the weather will last. You can also set how long the weather should last before the game returns to its normal weather programming.

If you use the /weather rain command in the desert, you won't see any rain. But if you move just one block into another biome, it will be raining there.

Syntax

```
/weather <clear|rain|thunder> [number of
seconds]
```

- Replace <clear|rain|thunder> with one of the three options: clear, rain, or thunder.

- May replace [number of seconds] with a number from 1 to 1000000 to set how many seconds (in real time) the weather lasts.

Examples

```
/weather clear 1000000
/weather thunder
```

The /worldborder Commands

There are eight /worldborder commands. A world border is a boundary to the edge of a Minecraft world. World borders are used by mapmakers for special maps or for mini-games, like an Ultra Hardcore game. Sometimes regular multiplayer servers will use a world border at the start of a new map so that players build close together for a while and get to know each other. The world border is a square boundary, with its default center at 0,0, that limits players to play within it. This command refers to the length of the radius of the border (though the world border is a square). This is the distance from the center of the world border to one of the four side edges. World borders can also be set to grow or reduce in size. A static world border is aqua. An expanding border is green, and a contracting one is red.

If you accidentally create a world border, you can remove it by setting the worldborder to 30000000 (30 million).

/worldborder add

The /worldborder add command lets you increase the size of the current world border. You can also set how many seconds it will take to expand from the current border to the new border.

Syntax

```
/worldborder add <blocks>[seconds]
```

- Replace <blocks> with the number of blocks you are adding.
- Replace [seconds] with the number of seconds (in real time) the expansion should take.

Example

```
/worldborder add 100 3600
```

/worldborder center

The /worldborder center command lets you specify the center of the world border square. The default center is 0,0.

Syntax

```
/worldborder center <x><y>
```

- Replace <x> and <y> with the X and Y coordinates of the new center. Because world borders cover the whole height of the map, you do not need to set the Z coordinate.

Example

```
/worldborder center 100 -100
```

/worldborder damage amount

By default, a world border gives .2 points of damage to a player for each block the player goes beyond the border's buffer zone. This command allows you to specify how many damage points are given per block.

Syntax

```
/worldborder damage amount <damage points>
```

- Replace <damage points> with the number of damage points a player will be dealt for each block he or she goes beyond the buffer.

Example

```
/worldborder damage amount 1
```

/worldborder damage buffer

The default buffer zone for a world border is five blocks, and players aren't damaged until they get beyond this. This command lets you change how many blocks deep, or beyond the border, the buffer zone is.

Syntax

```
/worldborder damage buffer <blocks>
```

- Replace <blocks> with the new size, in blocks, of the buffer.

Example

```
/worldborder damage buffer 3
```

/worldborder get

The /worldborder get command displays the size of the world border.

Syntax

```
/worldborder get
```

There are no additional parameters for this command, you just type /worldborder get.

/worldborder set

The worldborder set command lets you create a world border with a specific size. You can also set how many seconds it takes for the border to grow or retreat to the new size.

Syntax

```
/worldborder set <sizeInBlocks>[seconds]
```

- Replace <sizeInBlocks> with the radius size you want. An entire side's length of the world border will be double this, so if you set a radius of 500, the new world border will make a play zone of 1000x1000.

- May replace [seconds] with the time, in real-time seconds, that it will take the current world border to change to the new size. (An hour is 3600 seconds.)

Example

```
/worldborder set 500 7200
```

Minecraft warns players about the world border by turning their screen red if they get close.

/worldborder warning distance

A world border will by default give a player a visual warning—the screen tints red—when they are within 5 blocks. This command allows you to set a different warning distance.

Syntax

```
/worldborder warning distance <sizeInBlocks>
```

- Replace <sizeInBlocks> with the distance from the border, in blocks, that a player will be warned.

Example
```
/worldborder warning distance 15
```

/worldborder warning time

If a world border is decreasing, and will reach a player within 15 seconds, that player will receive a warning. This command allows you to change the 15-second world border warning time.

Syntax

```
/worldborder warning time <seconds>
```

- Replace <seconds> with the amount of warning time a player should get for an approaching world border.

Examples

```
/worldborder warning time 120
```

CHAPTER 7

BLOCK COMMANDS

Block commands act on blocks. Blocks include all of the square cubes you can place in the world, from acacia wood planks to zombie heads. They also include crafted objects that you can place, like ladders and anvils. Block commands include:

/blockdata
/clone
/fill
/replaceitem
/setblock

The /blockdata Command

Some blocks have data tags to describe special attributes they have, beyond what type of block they are and their XYZ coordinates. Different blocks have different data tags. For example, a flowerpot has a data tag to describe if it's holding a flower or plant and what that plant is.

Syntax

`/blockdata <x y z> <dataTag>`

- Replace <x y z> with the coordinates of the block you are changing.
- Replace <dataTag> with the dataTag(s) you are changing. You have to use attribute-value pairs, for example: {Item:sapling}

Example

`/blockdata ~ ~ ~1 {Item:sapling,Data:2}`

The example command adds a spruce sapling to the flowerpot 1 block away.

The /clone command lets you copy blocks in a 3D area to another area. This is a terrific command for making copies of something that was hard to build, like a house or a complicated wall. You do have to be careful in figuring out the coordinates. You have to choose two opposite corner blocks of the area you are copying. Then, when you clone the area, you choose just one block for the destination location. The block you choose will be the lowest northwest corner of the new location. You won't be able to rotate your copy or make it face a different direction. You are also limited to a total number of 4,096 blocks to clone.

Syntax

```
/clone <x1 y1 z1> <x2 y2 z2> <x y z>
[maskMode] [cloneMode] [TileName]
```

- Replace <x1 y1 z1> with the XYZ coordinates at one corner of the area you are copying.

- Replace <x2 y2 z2> with the XYZ coordinates of the opposite area you are copying.

- Replace <x y z> with the XYZ coordinates of the location destination. The block you choose will be the lowest northwest corner of your copied area.

- May replace [maskMode] with one of the following:

  ○ **filtered:** You use this with the [Tilename] parameter to say which type of block should be copied. So you could copy only stone blocks, for example.

- - **masked:** This copies only blocks that are not air blocks.
  - **replace:** This copies all blocks. This is the default maskMode.
- May replace [cloneMode] with one of the following:

  - **force:** This allows cloning to an overlapping area.
  - **move:** This will fill the original area you are cloning with air blocks.
  - **normal:** This is the default.

- If you are using the maskMode filtered, you must replace [TileName] with the ID name of the block type you want cloned.

The /clone command is a great way to make copies of buildings, like village houses, quickly.

Example

```
/clone -778 64 307 -774 68 310 -778 64 314
/clone -778 64 307 -774 68 310 ~2 ~ ~2
filtered normal sandstone
```

With the /fill command, you select a three-dimensional area and fill it with the block of your choice!

Syntax

`/fill <x1 y1 z1> <x2 y2 z2> <TileName> [dataValue] [oldBlockHandling] [dataTag] [replaceTileName] [replaceDataValue]`

- Replace <x1 y1 z1> and <x2 y2 z2> with the two opposite corners of your area.

- Replace <TileName> with the block ID name of the block you are using to fill the area.

- May replace [dataValue] with the data value for the block you are using.

- May replace [oldBlock Handling] with one of the following:
  - **destroy:** This makes the replaced blocks drop as if they were mined.
  - **hollow:** This replaces only the outside edges of the area with the new block and fills the interior with air blocks.
  - **keep:** This replaces only air blocks in the region with the new block.
  - **outline:** This is the same as hollow, except the interior blocks aren't changed.
  - **replace:** This is the default and replaces all blocks.

- May replace [dataTag] with a data tag for the new block. You cannot use this if you are using [replaceTileName] or [replaceDataValue].

- May replace [replaceTileName] with the type of block to replace in the region. This means, for example, that you can specify only to replace stone brick blocks with cobblestone blocks. This works only when you are using the oldBlockHandling value replace.

- May replace [replaceDataValue] with the data value of the tile to be replaced. This works only when you are using the oldBlockHandling value replace.

You can use the /fill command with the destroy option to clear a large area AND get the mining drops from it. Be careful though, Minecraft has no "Undo" button.

Examples

```
/fill -480 69 180 -500 89 200 diamond_ore
/fill ~2 ~ ~2 ~12 ~-5 ~12 air 0 destroy
```

This command modifies inventories of chests and players. You can use it to give items to players, refill dungeon chests, or equip mobs with weapons!

Syntax

`/replaceitem block <x> <y> <z> <slot> <item> [amount] [data] [dataTag]`

This runs the command in block mode, which modifies chests, furnaces, and any block with an inventory.

You can also run it in entity mode, which modifies the inventories of players or mobs:

`/replaceitem entity <selector> <slot> <item> [amount] [data] [dataTag]`

- In block mode, replace <x>, <y>, and <z> with the coordinates of the block you want to modify.

- In entity mode, replace <selector> with the player name or target selector of the entity you want to modify

- Replace <slot> with the number of the inventory slot you want to replace. Slot numbers for chests start at 0 in the top left corner and increase from left to right. Slot numbers for players are a little more complex.

- May replace [oldBlockHandling] with one of the following:

  ○ For inventory slots, use slot.inventory. *slot_number*, where slot_number is the number from 0 to 26 of the slot you want to modify.

○ For slots on the toolbar, use slot.hotbar. *slot_number*, where slot_number is the number from 0 to 8 of the slot you want to modify.

○ For armor slots, use slot.armor.chest, slot. armor.head, slot.armor.feet, and slot.armor. legs. These don't need numbers.

- Replace <item> with the item name of the block you want to replace.

- May replace <amount> with the amount of blocks you want to replace.

- May replace [data] and [dataTag] with the damage value and data tag of the block you want to replace.

Examples

```
/replaceitem block ~2 ~ ~ 0 minecraft:
diamond_sword
```

Replace the first slot in a chest next to you with a new diamond sword.

```
/replaceitem entity @a slot.hotbar.8
minecraft:stone 64
```

Replace the last item in each players toolbar with a stack of stone. Useful for building!

This command changes a specific block in the world into a different type of block.

Syntax

```
/setblock <x y z> <TileName> [dataValue]
[oldBlockHandling] [dataTag]
```

- Replace <x y z> with the XYZ coordinates of the block you are changing.

- Replace <TileName> with the ID name of the new block.

- May replace [dataValue] with any data value that you need to specify the new block.

- May replace [oldBlockHandling] with one of the following:
  - **destroy:** This makes the old block drop as if it were mined.
  - **keep:** This will only change the block if it is an air block.
  - **replace:** This is the default.

- May replace [dataTag] with the data tag for the new block.

Example

```
/setblock -489 89 187 planks 3
```

(This will change the existing block at this location to a jungle block.)

CHAPTER 8

ENTITY COMMANDS

ntity commands are commands you can use on entities. Entities are moving objects in the Minecraft world, like players, mobs, minecarts, and arrows. (However, most of these entity-restricted commands do not work on vehicles or projectiles.) The reason that there are somewhat different commands for the many types of Minecraft objects is because the objects in the various categories are programmed a bit differently. They have different abilities, and entities are much more complicated than most static blocks. A wolf, for example, can be "angry" (hostile), but it can also be tamed and have a collar, and you can breed it for more wolf cubs. A dirt block is pretty much just a dirt block.

Entity commands include:

/effect
/entitydata
/execute
/kill

```
/particle
/spreadplayers
/summon
/tp
```

The /effect Command

The /effect command lets you put status effects on entities (and remove effects from them), including players. For example, you can put the Blindness effect on any player entering a dark dungeon in a map you have made. Even if the player has torches, these won't help much. Look at Appendix E for a list of status effects.

Someone with the Blindness effect can still see, but only a few blocks around them. Even if it's daylight or there are torches, everything else is black.

Syntax

```
/effect <player> <effect> [seconds]
[amplifier] [hideParticles]
```

- Replace <player> with a player's username or a target selector.

- Replace <effect> with the ID name for the status effect you want.

- May replace [seconds] with the time in seconds of how long the effect should last.

- May replace [amplifier] with the "strength" of the effect, from 0 (the lowest strength) to 255.

- May replace [hideParticles] with true or false (the default is "false"). Selecting "true" will hide the swirly particle effects from the status effect.

To remove effects use:

```
/effect <player> clear
```

Examples

```
/effect @p fire_resistance 120 2 [hideparticles]
/effect @a clear
```

The /entitydata Command

With this command, you can change data tags for an entity. For example, you can add items to a chest, change what type of armor an entity is wearing, and more.

Syntax

```
/entitydata <entity> <dataTag>
```

- Replace <entity> with a target selector for an entity.

- Replace <dataTag> with one or more dataTags and their new values.

Example

Change slimes into huge high-jumpers with the /entitydata command.

```
/entitydata @e[type=Slime]
{Motion:[0.0,1.0,0.0],Size:20}
```

The /execute Command

The /execute command is used to run commands as if another entity had run them. It can also be used to execute a command for many entities at once. /execute is a very advanced command and has many parts.

Syntax

```
/execute <entity><x><y><z><command>
```

You can also run it in detect mode, which will check for a block near the entity and only run if that block is present:

```
/execute <entity><x><y><z> detect
<x2><y2><z2><block><data><command>
```

In addition to the entity name and the XYZ coordinates, this command uses several data tags:

- Replace <entity> with an entity name or target selector.

- Replace X, Y, and Z with relative or absolute coordinates.

- Replace <command> with the command you want to run.

- In detect mode, replace X2, Y2, and Z2 with with relative or absolute coordinates.

- In detect mode, replace <block> and <data> with a block ID and data tag, or just -1 to match all.

Examples

Summon a slime on top of all existing slimes:

```
/execute @e[type=Slime] ~ ~1 ~
/summon Slime ~ ~ ~
```

Create a pool of water under all thrown snowballs:

```
/execute @e[type=Snowball] ~ ~-4 ~ /fill ~-2
~ ~-2 ~2 ~ ~2 minecraft:water 0 replace air
```

The /kill Command

This is a simple command to kill (remove) any entity, including minecarts, boats, and mobs.

Syntax

```
/kill [player|entity]
```

- With command blocks, you must replace [player| entity] with a player's name or a target selector. With the Chat window, this is optional, and typing in just /kill will kill yourself. (This can actually be handy in Creative mode—you return to your spawn quickly. Because you are in Creative, it's easy to replace your inventory items.)

Examples

```
/kill meganfair
/kill @e[type=Zombie]
/kill @e[type=!Player]
```

The /particle Command

The /particle Command allows you to create particle effects at a specified location in the world. You used to be able to target players and entities with this command, but this feature is not present in Minecraft 1.9. There is a workaround with the /execute command, covered later in this chapter.

Using a value higher than 1 for the speed of a mobSpell effect will create multicolored swirls.

Syntax

```
/particle <name> <x y z> <xd yd zd>
<speed> [count] [mode]
```

- Replace <name> with the particle ID name.

- Replace <x y z> with the coordinates of the location you want the particle effect.

- Replace <xd yd zd> with size of the area to spawn the particles: how wide (along the X axis), how tall (along the Y axis), and how wide again (along the Z axis). Using 1 1 1 here will spawn the particles in a one-block cube. (However, many of these effects use a wider area, regardless.) Also, for the reddust, mobSpell, and mobSpell Ambient, the values here will actually change the color if the [count] argument is 0 or not included.

- Replace <speed> with a number of 0 (the lowest speed) or higher to increase the speed. Generally, the faster the speed, the shorter the time you can see the effect, so slower speeds, like 0 or 0.05 are good.

- May replace [count] with a number from 0 (1 particle) up, for the total number of particles in the effect. Watch out for really high numbers here, because that can lag or even crash Minecraft. On my PC, numbers around a million started a lag for the happy villager effect, but your mileage may vary.

- May replace [mode] with either "normal" or "force" to make the particles visible by players who have set particles to be minimal in their video options. The default is "normal."

Examples

```
/particle happyVillager ~2 ~ ~2 1 1 1 .05 1000
/particle mobSpell ~2 ~1 ~ 2 3 1 1 5000
```

This command will teleport a number of players into an area, all a certain distance from each other. Useful for spawning players in a mini-game!

Syntax

```
/spreadplayers <x> <z> <spreadDistance>
<maxRange> <respectTeams> <player...>
```

- Replace <x> and <z> with the coordinates of the center of the area you want players to teleport into.

- Replace <spreadDistance> with the minimum distance players can be from each other. Must be a positive number.

- Replace <maxRange> with the radius of the teleport area.

- Replace <respectTeams> with true or false. If you set it to true, it will group players by team. If not, it will be a free-for-all!

- Replace <player...> with one or more player names or a target selector. You can also target entities with this command.

Examples

```
/spreadplayers 0 0 1 10 false @a
```

The /summon Command

You can summon mobs riding on top of other mobs, like this stack of slimes on top of smaller slimes.

The /summon command is a great command to play with. You can create any Minecraft entity, and even some hidden mobs you don't see in the game, like skeleton horses. When you are changing things like data tags, to give a mob enchanted armor, for example, managing the brackets correctly can be hard.

Syntax

`/summon <EntityName> [x] [y] [z] [dataTag]`

- Replace <EntityName> with the entity ID name.

- May replace [x y z] with the coordinates to summon the entity to.

- May replace [dataTag] with a data tag that is appropriate for the entity.

Examples

To summon three slimes of increasing sizes, each one riding on top of the next smallest:

```
summon Slime ~ ~2 ~
{Size:3,Passengers:[{id:"Slime",
Size:5,Passengers:[{id:"Slime",Size:7}]}]}
```

To summon a villager that will give you a diamond for each block of dirt you give him:

```
/summon Villager ~1 ~ ~
{Offers:{Recipes:[{buy:{id:dirt,Count:1},sell:
{id:diamond,Count:1},rewardExp:false}]}}
```

You can create all types of customized entities, such as this tamed zombie horse, using the /summon command.

To create a tame zombie horse with a saddle, ready to ride:

```
/summon EntityHorse ~0 ~1 ~0
{Type:3,Tame:1,SaddleItem:{id:saddle}}
```

To create an overpowered zombie with 200 health points that can cause 15 points of damage:

```
/summon Zombie ~0 ~1 ~0 {Attributes:
[{Name:generic.maxHealth,Base:200},
{Name:generic.attackDamage,Base:15}],
Health:200.0f}
```

Using /summon for Fireworks

You can use the /summon command to create amazing fireworks displays. Here's an example:

```
/summon    FireworksRocketEntity   ~    ~5 ~
{LifeTime:20,   Fire-
worksItem:{id:401,Count:1,tag:
{Fireworks:{Explosions: [{Type:1,Flick-
er:1,Trail:1,Colors: [2516601],FadeCol-
ors:[3932152]}]}}}}
```

In addition to the entity name and the XYZ coordinates, this command uses several data tags:

- **Lifetime:** The number of seconds before the fireworks explosion

- Fireworks item {id:401,Count:1}, which also has tags

  - **Flicker** (true or false): for the twinkle effect
  - **Trail** (true or false): for the diamond trail effect
  - **Type**: for the shape of the explosion
  - **Colors**: for the color(s) the effect can be
  - **FadeColors**: for the colors to use as the image fades away

As you can see, nested data tags (one inside the other) make for a complicated series of brackets. And this is just one firework; you can have many inside the same command. Notice the color selection, too, uses a special format that is difficult to create. To make creating your own fireworks easier, you can use an online generator, where you can pick the shapes and colors and timing and just copy and paste the result into your own command block. One generator is at: www.minecraftupdates.com/fireworks. You can also just use a Minecraft color generator to pick your colors, like this one at http://wyattmarks.com/scripts/colorgenerator.

The /tp Command lets you or another player or entity instantly teleport somewhere in your world. You can teleport either to wherever another player is or to a specific set of coordinates. You can use command blocks to set up a teleportation hub that has buttons to teleport you to all your favorite locations.

Syntax

To send a player to the location of another player or entity:

`/tp [target player] <destination player>`

To send a player to a specific coordinate location:

`/tp [target player] <x y z> [<y-rot> <x-rot>]`

In command blocks, you must replace [target player] with a player's name or a target selector. You will teleport yourself if you are omitting this and using the Chat window.

- Replace <destination player> with the destination player's name or a target selector.

- Replace <x y z> with the coordinates of the destination.

- May replace <y-rot> with the number of degrees of rotation horizontally (180 (to face north), -90 (east), 0 (south), 90 (west)) and <x-rot> with the number of degrees of vertical rotation (90 is facing down, -90 is facing up).

Examples

```
/tp 0 64 0
/tp meganfair megorniuspi
/tp meganfair ~10 ~ ~10 180 90
```

CHAPTER 9

PLAYER COMMANDS

Player commands work on target players. Players are a type of entity in the game programming, so you can use most entity commands on players as well. However, you can't use all player commands on entities, because not all entities are players! There are some great player commands: /give lets you give any item to a player, including weapons enchanted with higher levels than possible in the regular game.

Player commands include:

/enchant
/give
/playsound
/spawnpoint
/xp

The /enchant Command

With the /enchant command, you can enchant armor, weapons, and tools. You can only enchant one item at a time, and the item has to be in the player's hand (selected in his or her inventory). You have to stick to enchantments that are possible in the regular game though, so you can't enchant a sword with Sharpness X (10). To give a custom enchantment like that, use the /give command.

Syntax

`/enchant <player> <enchantment ID> [level]`

- Replace <player> with a player's name or target selector.

- Replace <enchantment ID> with the enchantment's ID name or number (See Appendix D for a list of enchantment IDs.)

- May replace [level] with the level of enchantment. The limit is 5, 4, 3, or 1 for many enchantments.

While the enchantments in the game use Roman numerals (like Sharpness III), here you use a regular numeral (like 1 or 3) for the level.

Examples

```
/enchant meganfair silk_touch
/enchant @p 61 3
```

The /give Command

The /give command lets you give any Minecraft item or block to a player. Because you can use data tags to modify the item you are giving, you can use this command to give items that are enchanted to a higher level than possible in the game.

Syntax

```
/give <player> <item> [amount] [data]
[dataTag]
```

- Replace <player> with a player's name or a target selector.
- Replace <item> with the block ID name or item ID name you are giving.
- May replace [amount] with the number of the item you want to give.
- May replace [data] with a data value to specify the item (for example, if you are using spruce planks instead of oak, you will need to use the data value 1).
- May replace [dataTag] with a valid data tag for the item.

With the /give command, you can give items that are enchanted with levels much higher than allowed in the game.

Examples

```
/give @a cookie 10 0
/give MegorniusPI golden_apple 1 0
{display:{Name:Apple O Life}}

/give @p golden_sword 1 0 {ench:[{id:16,lvl 7},
{id:20,lvl:5},{id:19,lvl:5}],display:
{Name:"Creepa Killa",Lore:[Burn Creepers
and Hurl Them!]}}
```

The /playsound Command

With the /playsound command, you can play one of the sounds in Minecraft to another player. For example, if you have a command block with a particle effect of an explosion going off at a fort, you could add a sound effect of the explosion with another command block. You can find a list of these sounds on the Minecraft Wiki at http://minecraft.gamepedia.com/Sounds.json#Sound_events. Some of these sound events have several different sounds that are played randomly. For example, a ghast has seven different moaning sounds, all associated with the sound event mob.ghast.moan.

Syntax

`/playsound <sound> <player> [x y z] [volume] [pitch] [minimumVolume]`

- Replace <sound> with the name of the Minecraft sound event. (These are in the format category. sound.name; for example, mob.endermen.scream.)

- Replace <player> with a player's name or a target selector.

- May replace <x y z> with the location for the origin of the sound.

- May replace [volume] with a number from 0.0 up. The default is 1.0. Numbers under 1.0 are quieter and don't carry as far. For numbers above the 1.0 range, the sound carries farther.

- May replace [pitch] with a number that raises or lowers the pitch. 1.0 is the default, and numbers below this lower the pitch. Numbers above this raise the pitch.

- May replace [minimumVolume] with a number between 0 and 1 to represent how loud the sound is for players that aren't within the normal range for the sound.

Examples

```
/playsound mob.endermen.scream @p
/playsound mob.ghast.moan meganfair ~ ~ ~
1 0.1
```

Minecraft has a long list of sounds you can play with the /playsound command, including the sound of a player burping while they eat.

The /spawnpoint Command

With /spawnpoint you can set your or another player's spawn point in the world.

Syntax

`/spawnpoint [player] [x y z]`

- Must replace [player] with a player's name or a target selector if you are using command blocks. If not, you can omit this and the command will change your own spawn point.

- May replace [x y z] with the coordinates for the new spawn point. If you don't include this, the spawn point will be wherever the command is issued.

Examples

```
/spawnpoint @p ~ ~ ~
/spawnpoint MegorniusPI 500 64 -345
```

- - - - - - - - - - - - - - - -

The /xp command lets you give XP points or XP levels to any player.

Syntax

For points:

`/xp <amount> [player]`

For levels:

`/xp <amount>L [player]`

- Replace <amount> with the number of points or levels of XP you are giving.

- Use "L" after the <amount> (with no space before) to make this XP levels rather than points.

- Must replace [player] with a player name or target selector if you are using command blocks. Otherwise this is optional, and if you omit it, then you will get the XP points or levels.

Examples

```
/xp 30L @p
/xp 300 meganfair
```

APPENDIX A

BLOCK IDs

locks are objects that are placed in the Minecraft world, like cobblestone and wool blocks, as opposed to items that you use, like swords and gold ingots.

This Block ID list is a shortened list taken from the Minecraft Wiki reference and is up to date as of version 1.9. The full block ID list at the Wiki is at minecraft.gamepedia.com/Data_values/ Block_IDs. Data values lists are at minecraft.gamepedia.com/ Data_values. If there is a block whose ID you need that isn't on this list, visit the Minecraft Wiki. The Wiki is a fantastic public resource for all things Minecraft and is translated into many languages.

Some blocks in the same category share a block name and a block ID number. For example, blocks for stone, granite, diorite, and andesite all have the same name "stone" and the same ID "1". When you want to refer to any of these except for the default stone, you will need to include its data value (DV) number.

Also, you will find that some blocks seem categorized oddly. Because Minecraft is a continually changing game, the tactics used by developers for naming and categorizing blocks has also changed a little over time. So while Acacia Wood Stairs has its own ID name and number, Acacia Wood and Acacia Wood Planks share an ID name and number with other types of wood.

Building Blocks

	Block	ID Name	ID #	DV
	Acacia Wood Stairs	acacia_stairs	163	
	Acacia/Dark Oak Wood	log2 Variant data values: Dark Oak Wood: 1	162	*
	Bedrock	bedrock	7	
	Birch Wood Stairs	birch_stairs	135	
	Brick	brick_block	45	
	Brick Stairs	brick_stairs	108	
	Clay	clay	82	

	Coal Block	coal_block	173	
	Coal Ore	coal_ore	16	
	Cobblestone	cobblestone	4	
	Cobblestone Stairs	stone_stairs	67	
	Dark Oak Wood Stairs	dark_oak_stairs	164	
	Diamond Block	diamond_block	57	
	Diamond Ore	diamond_ore	56	
	Dirt	dirt Variant data values: Coarse Dirt: 1; Podzol: 2	3	*
	Emerald Ore	emerald_ore	129	
	Emerald Block	emerald_block	133	
	End Stone	end_stone	121	
	Glass	glass	20	
	Glowstone	glowstone	89	
	Gold Block	gold_block	41	
	Gold Ore	gold_ore	14	
	Grass Block	grass	2	
	Gravel	gravel	13	
	Hardened Clay	hardened_clay	172	

	Ice	ice	79	
	Iron Block	iron_block	42	
	Iron Ore	iron_ore	15	
	Jungle Wood Stairs	jungle_stairs	136	
	Lapis Lazuli Block	lapis_block	22	
	Lapis Lazuli Ore	lapis_ore	21	
	Moss Stone	mossy_cobblestone	48	
	Mycelium	mycelium	110	
	Nether Brick	nether_brick	112	
	Nether Quartz Ore	quartz_ore	153	
	Netherrack	netherrack	87	
	Oak Wood Stairs	oak_stairs	53	
	Obsidian	obsidian	49	
	Packed Ice	packed_ice	174	
	Prismarine	prismarine Variant data values: Prismarine bricks (1); Dark Prismarine (2)	168	*
	Quartz Block	quartz_block Variant data values: Chiseled Quartz (1); Pillar Quartz (2)	155	*
	Quartz Stairs	quartz_stairs	156	

	Red Sandstone	red_sandstone Variant data values: Chiseled Red Sandstone: 1; Smooth Red Sandstone: 2	179	
	Red Sandstone Slab	stone_slab2	182	
	Red Sandstone Stairs	red_sandstone_stairs	180	
	Redstone Block	redstone_block	152	
	Redstone Ore	redstone_ore	73	
	Sand	sand Variant data values: Red sand: 1	12	0
	Sandstone	sandstone Variant data values: Chiseled Sandstone: 1; Smooth Sandstone: 2.	24	
	Sandstone Stairs	sandstone_stairs	128	
	Sea Lantern	sea_lantern	169	
	Snow (block)	snow	80	
	Soul Sand	soul_sand	88	
	Spruce Wood Stairs	spruce_stairs	134	
	Stained Clay	stained_hardened_clay Variant data values: Orange: 1; Magenta: 2; Light Blue: 3; Yellow: 4; Lime: 5; Pink: 6; Gray: 7; Light Gray: 8; Cyan: 9; Purple: 10; Blue: 11; Brown: 12; Green: 13; Red: 14; and Black: 15	159	*

	Stained Glass (white)	stained_glass Variant data values: Orange: 1; Magenta: 2; Light Blue: 3; Yellow: 4; Lime: 5; Pink: 6; Gray: 7; Light Gray: 8; Cyan: 9; Purple: 10; Blue: 11; Brown: 12; Green: 13; Red: 14; and Black: 15	95	*
	Stained Glass Pane	stained_glass_pane Variant data values: Orange: 1; Magenta: 2; Light Blue: 3; Yellow: 4; Lime: 5; Pink: 6; Gray: 7; Light Gray: 8; Cyan: 9; Purple: 10; Blue: 11; Brown: 12; Green: 13; Red: 14; and Black: 15	160	*
	Stone	stone Variant data values: Granite: 1; Polished Granite: 2; Diorite: 3; Polished Diorite: 4: Andesite: 5; Polished Andesite: 6	1	*
	Stone Brick	stonebrick Variant data values: Mossy Stone Brick: 1; Cracked Stone Brick: 2; Chiseled Stone Brick: 3	98	*
	Stone Brick Stairs	stone_brick_stairs	109	
	Stone Slab	stone_slab Variant data values: Sandstone Slab:1; Wooden Slab: 2; Cobblestone Slab:3; Brick Slab: 4; Stone Brick Slab: 5; Nether Brick Slab: 6; Quartz Slab: 7	44	*

	Block	ID Name	ID #	DV
	Wood (Oak)	log Variant data values: Spruce: 1; Birch: 2; Jungle: 3; Acacia: 4; Dark Oak: 5	17	*
	Wood Planks (Oak)	planks Variant data values: Spruce: 1; Birch: 2; Jungle: 3; Acacia: 4; Dark Oak: 5	5	*
	Wooden Slab (Oak)	wooden_slab Variant data values: Spruce: 1; Birch: 2; Jungle: 3; Acacia: 4; Dark Oak: 5	126	*
	Wool	wool Variant data values: Orange: 1; Magenta: 2; Light Blue: 3; Yellow: 4; Lime: 5; Pink: 6; Gray: 7; Light Gray: 8; Cyan: 9; Purple: 10; Blue: 11; Brown: 12; Green: 13; Red: 14; and Black: 15	35	*

Decoration Blocks

	Block	ID Name	ID #	DV
	Bookshelf	bookshelf	47	
	Carpet (white)	carpet Variant data values: Orange: 1; Magenta: 2; Light Blue: 3; Yellow: 4; Lime: 5; Pink: 6; Gray: 7;	171	

	Block	ID Name	ID#	DV
		Light Gray: 8; Cyan: 9; Purple: 10; Blue: 11; Brown: 12; Green: 13; Red: 14; and Black: 15		
	Cobweb	web	30	
	Flower Pot	flower_pot	140	
	Glass Pane	glass_pane	102	
	Hay Bale	hay_block	170	
	Iron Bars	iron_bars	101	
	Mob head (skeleton)	skull Variant data values: Wither skeleton: 1; Zombie: 2; Steve: 3; Creeper: 4.	144	
	Snow (layer)	snow_layer	78	

Fences, Gates, and Doors

	Block	ID Name	ID#	DV
	Acacia Door	acacia_door	196	
	Acacia Fence	acacia_fence	192	
	Acacia Fence Gate	acacia_fence_gate	187	
	Birch Door	birch_door	194	

	Birch Fence	birch_fence	189	
	Birch Fence Gate	birch_fence_gate	184	
	Cobblestone Wall	cobblestone_wall For a mossy cobble wall, use data value 1	139	
	Dark Oak Door	dark_oak_door	197	
	Dark Oak Fence	dark_oak_fence	191	
	Dark Oak Fence Gate	dark_oak_fence_gate	186	
	Fence (oak)	fence	85	
	Fence Gate (oak)	fence_gate	107	
	Jungle Door	jungle_door	195	
	Jungle Fence	jungle_fence	190	
	Jungle Fence Gate	jungle_fence_gate	185	
	Nether Brick Fence	nether_brick_fence	113	
	Nether Brick Stairs	nether_brick_stairs	114	
	Spruce Door	spruce_door	193	
	Spruce Fence	spruce_fence	188	
	Spruce Fence Gate	spruce_fence_gate	183	
	Wood Door (oak)	wooden_door	64	

Miscellaneous

	Block	ID Name	ID #	DV
–	Air	air	0	
	Anvil	anvil	145	
	Barrier	barrier	166	
	Bed	bed	26	
	Brewing Stand	brewing_stand	117	
	Cake	cake	92	
	Cauldron	cauldron	118	
	Chest	chest	54	
	Command Block	command_block	137	
	Crafting Table	crafting_table	58	
	Enchantment Table	enchanting_table	116	
	Furnace	furnace	61	
	Jukebox	jukebox	84	
	Note Block	noteblock	25	
	Piston	piston	33	
	Slime Block	slime	165	
	Sponge	sponge Variant data value: Wet Sponge: 1	19	

	Block	ID Name	ID #	
	TNT	tnt	46	
	Torch	torch	50	

Plant Material

	Block	ID Name	ID #	DV
	Acacia/Dark Oak Leaves	leaves2 Variant data values: Dark Oak: 1	161	*
	Allium	red_flower	38	2
	Azure Bluet	red_flower	38	3
	Blue Orchid	red_flower	38	1
	Brown Mushroom	brown_mushroom	39	
	Brown Mushroom (block)	brown_mushroom_block	99	
	Cactus	cactus	81	
	Cocoa	cocoa	127	
	Dandelion	yellow_flower	37	
	Dead Bush	deadbush	32	
	Double Tallgrass	double_plant	175	2
	Fern	tallgrass	31	2

	Grass	tallgrass	31	1
	Jack o'Lantern	lit_pumpkin	91	
	Large Fern	double_plant	175	3
	Leaves (oak)	leaves Variant data values: 1-3: Spruce: 1; Birch: 2; Jungle: 3	18	*
	Lilac	double_plant	175	1
	Lily Pad	waterlily	111	
	Melon	melon_block	103	
	Nether Wart (block)	nether_wart	115	
	Orange Tulip	red_flower	38	5
	Oxeye Daisy	red_flower	38	8
	Peony	double_plant	175	5
	Pink Tulip	red_flower	38	7
	Poppy	red_flower	38	0
	Pumpkin	pumpkin	86	
	Red Mushroom	red_mushroom	40	
	Red Mushroom (block)	red_mushroom_block	100	
	Red Tulip	red_flower	38	4
	Rose Bush	double_plant	175	4

	Sapling (Oak)	sapling Variant data values: Spruce: 1; Birch : 2; Jungle: 3; Acacia: 4; Dark Oak: 5	6	*
	Sugar Cane (block)	reeds	83	
	Sunflower	double_plant	175	
	Vines	vine	106	
	White Tulip	red_flower	38	6

ITEM IDs

Minecraft items are things that you use or wear, like tools and weapons, rather than place in the world (although some items are placeable, like brewing stands). While block ID numbers are all below 255, item ID numbers are all above 255. As with block IDs, some similar items, like different dyes, share the same ID number but have different data value IDs.

This is a shortened list taken from the Minecraft Wiki refer ence. The full item ID list at the Wiki is at minecraft.gamepedia. com/Data_values/Item_IDs. Data values lists are at minecraft. gamepedia.com/Data_values. If there is an item whose ID you need that isn't on this list, visit the Minecraft Wiki. In addition, some Minecraft objects have both block and item IDs.

	Item	ID Name	ID Number
	Armor Stand	armor_stand	416
	Chain Boots	chainmail_boots	305
	Chain Chestplate	chainmail_chestplate	303
	Chain Helmet	chainmail_helmet	302
	Chain Leggings	chainmail_leggings	304
	Diamond Boots	diamond_boots	313
	Diamond Chestplate	diamond_chestplate	311
	Diamond Helmet	diamond_helmet	310
	Diamond Leggings	diamond_leggings	312
	Golden Boots	golden_boots	317
	Golden Chestplate	golden_chestplate	315
	Golden Helmet	golden_helmet	314
	Golden Leggings	golden_leggings	316
	Horse Armor (Diamond)	diamond_horse_armor	419
	Horse Armor (Golden)	golden_horse_armor	418
	Horse Armor (Iron)	iron_horse_armor	417
	Iron Boots	iron_boots	309

	Item	ID Name	ID Number
	Iron Chestplate	iron_chestplate	307
	Iron Helmet	iron_helmet	306
	Iron Leggings	iron_leggings	308
	Leather Boots	leather_boots	301
	Leather Cap	leather_helmet	298
	Leather Pants	leather_leggings	300
	Leather Tunic	leather_chestplate	299

Food and Plant-related

	Item	ID Name	ID Number
	Apple	apple	260
	Baked Potato	baked_potato	393
	Beef (Raw)	beef	363
	Bread	bread	297
	Cake	cake	354
	Carrot	carrot	391
	Chicken (Raw)	chicken	365
	Chicken (Cooked)	cooked_chicken	366

	Cookie	cookie	357
	Fish (Raw)	fish	349
	Fish (Cooked)	cooked_fish	350
	Golden Apple	golden_apple	322
	Golden Carrot	golden_carrot	396
	Melon	melon	360
	Melon Seeds	melon_seeds	362
	Milk	milk_bucket	335
	Mushroom Stew	mushroom_stew	282
	Mutton (Cooked)	cooked_mutton	424
	Mutton (Raw)	mutton	423
	Porkchop (Cooked)	cooked_porkchop	320
	Porkchop (Raw)	porkchop	319
	Potato	potato	392
	Poisonous Potato	poisonous_potato	394
	Pumpkin Pie	pumpkin_pie	400
	Pumpkin Seeds	pumpkin_seeds	361
	Rabbit (Cooked)	cooked_rabbit	412
	Rabbit (Raw)	rabbit	411
	Rabbit Stew	rabbit_stew	413

	Item	ID Name	ID Number
	Rotten Flesh	rotten_flesh	367
	Seeds	wheat_seeds	295
	Steak	cooked_beef	364
	Sugar	sugar	353
	Wheat	wheat	296

Household and Miscellaneous Goods

	Item	ID Name	ID Number
	Banner	banner	425
	Bed	bed	355
	Birch Door	birch_door	428
	Boat	boat	333
	Book	book	340
	Book and Quill	writable_book	386
	Bottle o' Enchanting	experience_bottle	384
	Bowl	bowl	281
	Bucket	bucket	325
	Carrot on a Stick	carrot_on_a_stick	398

	Empty Map	map	395
	Enchanted Book	enchanted_book	403
	Fire Charge	fire_charge	385
–	Firework Rocket	fireworks	401
	Firework Star	firework_charge	402
	Glass Bottle	glass_bottle	374
	Iron Door	iron_door	330
	Item Frame	item_frame	389
	Jungle Door	jungle_door	429
	Minecart	minecart	328
	Oak Door	wooden_door	324
	Painting	painting	321
	Paper	paper	339
	Potion (Water Bottle) *For specific potions, see Appendix H: Potion IDs	potion	373
	Saddle	saddle	329
	Sign	sign	323
	Spawn Egg	spawn_egg	383
	Spruce Door	spruce_door	427
	Stick	stick	280

Materials and Mob Drops

	Item	ID Name	ID Number
	Blaze Powder	blaze_powder	377
	Blaze Rod	blaze_rod	369
	Bone	bone	352
	Brick	brick	336
	Clay	clay_ball	337
	Coal	coal	263
	Diamond	diamond	264
	Dye (Ink Sac) *bonemeal	dye	351
	Egg	egg	344
	Emerald	emerald	388
	Ender Pearl	ender_pearl	368
	Eye of Ender	ender_eye	381
	Feather	feather	288
	Fermented Spider Eye	fermented_ spider_eye	376
	Flint	flint	318
	Ghast Tear	ghast_tear	370
	Glistering Melon	speckled_melon	382

	Glowstone Dust	glowstone_dust	348
	Gold Ingot	gold_ingot	266
	Gold Nugget	gold_nugget	371
	Gunpowder	gunpowder	289
	Iron Ingot	iron_ingot	265
	Lava Bucket	lava_bucket	327
	Leather	leather	334
	Magma Cream	magma_cream	378
	Mob Head	skull	397
	Nether Brick	netherbrick	405
	Nether Quartz	quartz	406
	Nether Star	nether_star	399
	Nether Wart	nether_wart	372
	Prismarine Shard	prismarine_shard	409
	Prismarine Crystals	prismarine_crystals	410
	Rabbit's Foot	rabbit_foot	414
	Rabbit Hide	rabbit_hide	415
	Redstone	redstone	331
	Slimeball	slime_ball	341
	Snowball	snowball	332

	Item	ID Name	ID Number
	Spider Eye	spider_eye	375
	String	string	287
	Sugar Cane	reeds	338
	Water Bucket	water_bucket	326

Music Disc ID Names and Numbers

	Item	ID Name	ID Number
	11 Disc	record_11	2266
	13 Disc	record_13	2256
	Blocks Disc	record_blocks	2258
	Cat Disc	record_cat	2257
	Chirp Disc	record_chirp	2259
	Far Disc	record_far	2260
	Mall Disc	record_mall	2261
	Mellohi Disc	record_mellohi	2262
	Stal Disc	record_stal	2263
	Strad Disc	record_strad	2264
	Wait Disc	record_wait	2267
	Ward Disc	record_ward	2265

	Item	ID Name	ID Number
	Clock	clock	347
	Compass	compass	345
	Diamond Axe	diamond_axe	279
	Diamond Hoe	diamond_hoe	293
	Diamond Pickaxe	diamond_pickaxe	278
	Diamond Shovel	diamond_shovel	277
	Fishing Rod	fishing_rod	346
	Flint and Steel	flint_and_steel	259
	Golden Axe	golden_axe	286
	Golden Hoe	golden_hoe	294
	Golden Pickaxe	golden_pickaxe	285
	Golden Shovel	golden_shovel	284
	Iron Axe	iron_axe	258
	Iron Hoe	iron_hoe	292
	Iron Pickaxe	iron_pickaxe	257
	Iron Shovel	iron_shovel	256
	Lead	lead	420
	Name Tag	name_tag	421

	Shears	shears	359
	Stone Axe	stone_axe	275
	Stone Hoe	stone_hoe	291
	Stone Pickaxe	stone_pickaxe	274
	Stone Shovel	stone_shovel	273
	Wooden Axe	wooden_axe	271
	Wooden Hoe	wooden_hoe	290
	Wooden Pickaxe	wooden_pickaxe	270
	Wooden Shovel	wooden_shovel	269

Weapons

	Item	ID Name	ID Number
	Arrow	arrow	262
	Bow	bow	261
	Diamond Sword	diamond_sword	276
	Golden Sword	golden_sword	283
	Iron Sword	iron_sword	267
	Wooden Sword	wooden_sword	268

POTION IDs

All of these potions have the ID name "potion" and the ID number "373" so you use their data value to specify which potion you want. After the potion name is the length of time that the potion is in effect; otherwise the potion is instant.

Potion	Data Value
Awkward Potion	16
Fire Resistance Potion (3:00)	8195
Fire Resistance Potion (8:00)	8259
Fire Resistance Splash (2:15)	16387
Fire Resistance Splash (6:00)	16451
Harming Potion	8204

Harming Potion II	8236
Harming Splash	16396
Harming Splash II	16428
Healing Potion	8197
Healing Potion II	8229
Healing Splash	16389
Healing Splash II	16421
Invisibility Potion (3:00)	8206
Invisibility Potion (8:00)	8270
Invisibility Splash (2:15)	16398
Invisibility Splash (6:00)	16462
Leaping Potion (3:00)	8267
Leaping Potion II (1:30)	8235
Leaping Splash (2:15)	16459
Leaping Splash II (1:07)	16427
Night Vision Potion (3:00)	8198
Night Vision Potion (8:00)	8262
Night Vision Splash (2:15)	16390
Night Vision Splash (6:00)	16454
Poison Potion (0:45)	8196
Poison Potion (2:00)	8260
Poison Potion II (0:22)	8228
Poison Potion II (1:00)	8292
Poison Splash (0:33)	16388
Poison Splash (1:30)	16452
Poison Splash II (0:16)	16420
Poison Splash II (0:45)	16484
Regeneration Potion (0:45)	8193
Regeneration Potion (2:00)	8257
Regeneration Potion II (0:22)	8225
Regeneration Potion II (1:00)	8289

Regeneration Splash (0:33)	16385
Regeneration Splash (1:30)	16449
Regeneration Splash II (0:16)	16417
Regeneration Splash II (0:45)	16481
Slowness Potion (1:30)	8202
Slowness Potion (4:00)	8266
Slowness Splash (1:07)	16394
Slowness Splash (3:00)	16458
Strength Potion (3:00)	8201
Strength Potion (8:00)	8265
Strength Potion II (1:30)	8233
Strength Potion II (4:00)	8297
Strength Splash (2:15)	16393
Strength Splash (6:00)	16457
Strength Splash II (1:07)	16425
Strength Splash II (3:00)	16489
Swiftness Potion (3:00)	8194
Swiftness Potion (8:00)	8258
Swiftness Potion II (1:30)	8226
Swiftness Potion II (4:00)	8290
Swiftness Splash (2:15)	16386
Swiftness Splash (6:00)	16450
Swiftness Splash II (1:07)	16418
Swiftness Splash II (3:00)	16482
Water Breathing Potion (3:00)	8205
Water Breathing Potion (8:00)	8269
Water Breathing Splash (2:15)	16397
Water Breathing Splash (6:00)	16461
Weakness Potion (1:30)	8200
Weakness Potion (4:00)	8264
Weakness Splash (1:07)	16392
Weakness Splash (3:00)	16456

ENCHANTMENT IDs

These IDs are used with the /give command and the /enchant command. The Highest Level is the maximum level the enchantment can have in regular gameplay.

Enchantment	Name	ID	Highest Level
Protection	protection	0	IV
Fire Protection	fire_protection	1	IV
Feather Falling	feather_falling	2	IV
Blast Protection	blast_protection	3	IV
Projectile Protection	projectile_protection	4	IV
Respiration	respiration	5	III

Aqua Affinity	aqua_affinity	6	I
Thorns	thorns	7	III
Depth Strider	depth_strider	8	III
Sharpness	sharpness	16	V
Smite	smite	17	V
Bane of Arthropods	bane_of_arthropods	18	V
Knockback	knockback	19	II
Fire Aspect	fire_aspect	20	II
Looting	looting	21	III
Efficiency	efficiency	32	V
Silk Touch	silk_touch	33	I
Unbreaking	unbreaking	34	III
Fortune	fortune	35	III
Power	power	48	V
Punch	punch	49	II
Flame	flame	50	I
Infinity	infinity	51	I
Luck of the Sea	luck_of_the_sea	61	III
Lure	lure	62	III

STATUS EFFECTS

se these ID names or numbers for status effects with the /effect command.

	Status Effect	ID Name	ID #
	Speed	speed	1
	Slowness	slowness	2
	Haste	haste	3
	Mining Fatigue	mining_fatigue	4

	Strength	strength	5
−	Instant Health	instant_health	6
−	Instant Damage	instant_damage	7
	Jump Boost	jump_boost	8
	Nausea	nausea	9
	Regeneration	regeneration	10
	Resistance	resistance	11
	Fire Resistance	fire_resistance	12
	Water Breathing	water_breathing	13
	Invisibility	invisibility	14
	Blindness	blindness	15
	Night vision	night_vision	16
	Hunger	hunger	17
	Weakness	weakness	18
	Poison	poison	19
	Wither	wither	20
	Health Boost	health_boost	21
	Absorption	absorption	22
−	Saturation	saturation	23

PARTICLES

se these ID names for visual effects with the /particle command.

This is a shortened version of the full particle list at the Minecraft Wiki. For the full list, visit minecraft.gamepedia.com/Particles

angryVillager
bubble (only works
   underwater)
cloud
crit

dripWater
dripLava
droplet
enchantmenttable
explode

fireworksSpark

flame

happyVillager

heart

hugeexplosion

instantSpell

largeexplode

largesmoke

lava

magicCrit

mobSpell

note

portal

reddust

slime

smoke

snowballpoof

snowshovel

spell

splash

wake

witchMagic

APPENDIX G

ENTITY IDS

You refer to entities by their ID name, which is also called their Savegame ID. This is a slightly shortened list of the full entity ID list at the Minecraft Wiki, which you can find here: minecraft.gamepedia.com/Data_values/Entity_IDs

Entity	ID Name (Savegame ID)
Bat	Bat
Blaze	Blaze
Cave Spider	CaveSpider
Chicken	Chicken
Cow	Cow
Creeper	Creeper
Ender Dragon	EnderDragon

Entity	ID Name (Savegame ID)
Enderman	Enderman
Endermite	Endermite
Experience Orb	XPOrb
Falling Block (gravel, sand, anvil, dragon egg)	FallingSand
Firework Rocket	FireworksRocketEntity
Giant	Giant
Ghast	Ghast
Guardian	Guardian
Horse	EntityHorse
Iron Golem	VillagerGolem
Killer Rabbit	Rabbit
Magma Cube	LavaSlime
Mooshroom	MushroomCow
Ocelot	Ozelot
Pig	Pig
Primed TNT	PrimedTnt
Rabbit	Rabbit
Sheep	Sheep
Silverfish	Silverfish
Skeleton	Skeleton
Slime	Slime
Snow Golem	SnowMan
Spider	Spider
Squid	Squid
Villager	Villager
Witch	Witch
Wither	WitherBoss
Wolf	Wolf
Zombie Villager	Zombie
Zombie Pigman	PigZombie

APPENDIX H

COMMANDS

This list covers most Minecraft commands, but not server administration commands. To learn more about commands that manage a server, visit the Minecraft Wiki at minecraft.gamepedia.com/Commands.

Italics show the text that must be replaced. The angle brackets show parameters that must be included, and the square brackets show optional parameters. (These brackets shouldn't be included in the command.) Also, the commands and syntax below start with a slash. The slash is required for commands used in the Chat window but optional for commands used in a command block.

Command	Syntax
/achievement	`/achievement <give|take> <stat_name|*> [player]`
/blockdata	`/blockdata <x y z> <dataTag>`
/clear	`/clear [player] [item] [data] [maxCount] [dataTag]`
/clone	`/clone <x1 y1 z1> <x2 y2 z2> <x y z> [maskMode] [cloneMode] [TileName]`
/defaultgamemode	`/defaultgamemode <mode>`
/difficulty	`/difficulty <new difficulty>`

/effect	`/effect <player> <effect> [seconds] [amplifier] [hideParticles]`
	
	`/effect <player> clear`

/enchant	`/enchant <player> <enchantment ID> [level]`
/entitydata	`/entitydata <entity> <dataTag>`

/execute	`/execute <entity> <x y z> <command>`
	
	`/execute <entity> <x y z> detect <x2 y2 z2> <block> <data> <command>`

/fill	`/fill <x1 y1 z1> <x2 y2 <z2> <TileName> [dataValue] [oldBlockHandling] [dataTag]`
	
	`/fill <x1 y1 z1> <x2 y2 z2> <TileName> <dataValue> replace [replaceTileName] [replaceDataValue]`

/gamemode	`/gamemode <mode> [player]`

Command	Syntax
/gamerule	/gamerule <rule name> [value]
/give	/give <player> <item> [amount] [data] [dataTag]
/help	/help [page|command name] /? [page|command name]
/kill	/kill [player|entity]
/list	/list
/me	/me <action …>
/particle	/particle <name> <x y z> <xd yd zd> <speed> [count] [mode]
/playsound	/playsound <sound> <player> [x y z] [volume] [pitch] [minimumVolume]
/replaceitem	/replaceitem block <x y z> <slot> <item> [amount] [data] [dataTag] /replaceitem entity <selector> <slot> <item> [amount] [data] [dataTag]
/say	/say <message …>
/scoreboard	/scoreboard <objectives|players|teams> …
/seed	/seed
/setblock	/setblock <x y z> <TileName> [dataValue] [oldBlockHandling] [dataTag]
/setworldspawn	/setworldspawn [x y z]
/spawnpoint	/spawnpoint [player] [x y z]
/spreadplayers	/spreadplayers <x z> <spreadDistance> <maxRange> <respectTeams> <player …>

Command	Syntax
/stats	/stats block <x y z> clear <stat>
/stats block <x y z> set <stat> <selector><objective>
/stats entity <selector2> clear <stat>
/stats entity <selector2> set <stat> <selector> <objective>
/summon	/summon <EntityName> [x y z] [dataTag]
/tell	/tell <player> <private message ...>
/msg <player> <private message ...>
/w <player> <private message ...>
/tellraw	/tellraw <player> <raw json message>
/testfor	/testfor <player> [dataTag]
/testforblock	/testforblock <x y z> <TileName> [dataValue] [dataTag]
/testforblocks	/testforblocks <x1 y1 z1> <x2 y2 z2> <x y z> [mode]
/time	/time <add|query|set> <value>
/title	/title <player> clear
/title <player> reset
/title <player> subtitle <raw json title>
/title <player> times <fadeIn> <stay> <fadeOut>
/title <player> title <raw json title>

Command	Syntax
/toggledownfall	/toggledownfall
/tp	/tp [*target player*] <*destination player*> /tp [*target player*] <*x y z*> [<*y-rot x-rot*>]
/trigger	/trigger <*objective*> <add|set> <*value*>
/weather	/weather <clear|rain|thunder> [*duration in seconds*]
/worldborder	/worldborder add <*sizeInBlocks*> [*timeInSeconds*] /worldborder center <*x z*> /worldborder damage amount <*damagePerBlock*> /worldborder damage buffer <*sizeInBlocks*> /worldborder get /worldborder set <*sizeInBlocks*> [*timeInSeconds*] /worldborder warning distance <*blocks*> /worldborder warning time <*seconds*>
/xp	/xp <*amount*> [*player*] /xp <*amount*>L [*player*]

*Source: Minecraft Wiki at minecraft.gamepedia.com/Commands and the Minecraft 1.9 game.

REDSTONE

HACKS FOR MINECRAFTERS

INTRODUCTION

Redstone is one of the most amazing and complicated aspects to Minecraft. With it you can invent brand-new, working in-game machines, from an automatic door to a flying machine or calculator. Some of the most popular contraptions to make are:

- Automatic farms, to help harvest crops
- Mob farms, to gather and kill large numbers of mobs and get their drops
- Automatic doors
- Automatic lighting
- Item sorting and storage

Where Do You Get Redstone?

You get redstone by mining redstone ore at levels 16 and lower. Each block of ore will get you 4 or 5 redstone, and more if you are mining with a Fortune-enchanted pick. Witches sometimes will drop redstone when they die, and priest villagers may also trade it.

Redstone machines, or contraptions, have three main elements: devices, power, and the signal that transmits power to the device. A redstone device is an object that performs an action when it receives power. Redstone power comes from specific power source blocks, such as redstone blocks and torches. You can extend the reach of this power through trails of redstone dust.

Here is the one of the simplest redstone contraptions, a trap-door activated by a button.

This trapdoor is activated by a button on the next block.

The power source is the button, which gives out a temporary power signal when it is pressed. While that signal exists, the trapdoor opens. When the signal disappears, the trapdoor closes. You don't need any redstone dust if the power source is right against the device. However, if you want the button to be farther away from the trapdoor, you would have to connect the trapdoor and the button through redstone dust.

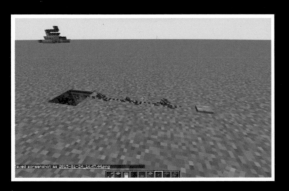

This button is placed farther away from the trapdoor, so you use redstone dust to carry its signal.

The best way to understand redstone is to learn by doing. When you read about the devices in the first three chapters, play around and hook them up together to see what happens. When you make one of the projects and it works, make it again and add your own changes to see what works and what doesn't.

Redstone dust and devices like torches, repeaters, and comparators can be uprooted by water, destroying contraptions. Make sure when you finish a contraption to protect it from accidental water placement by walling it off.

It is much easier to start learning redstone in Creative mode, where you have access to all items to play with. If you don't, each project has a complete list of components so you can gather these before beginning.

Placing blocks and items for a contraption can sometimes be tricky. In the projects, in order to place a block in a certain location, you may need to first place other temporary blocks that the first block can rest on. You'll want to remember to remove any temporary blocks, so it can help to choose a specific type of material for these blocks, like red wool.

Sometimes to place objects, like hoppers, on top of others, you may need to shift-right-click (holding the shift button while right-clicking). Some objects always place to face you (like pistons). You may need to move around a bit, or place some temporary blocks to stand in the right place, in order to place these correctly.

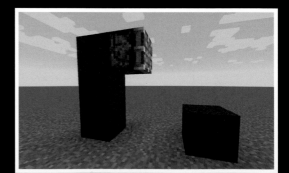

Use a special block, like red wool, for temporary blocks you use to stand on or to help place objects. This will help you remember to remove them later.

If you complete a project, but it isn't working the way you think it should, go through the steps to check if everything is in place and pointing in the right direction. Important first things to check when a contraption doesn't work include:

- Are repeaters, comparators, and redstone dust pointing in the right direction?

- Are any blocks being powered that shouldn't be?

- What isn't receiving power that should be?

- Is a redstone torch turning off a signal?

- Should any repeaters have delays?

Many of the contraptions in this book are based on mechanisms that other Minecraft players have created and shared online, in forums, or on video-sharing sites like YouTube. Making contraptions following other people's designs is a great way to start understanding redstone. However, you will start to understand even more when you take these contraptions apart, and put them back again slightly differently, to figure out exactly how they work.

Note: This book's projects were created in Minecraft 1.8.1 for PC and updated to reflect Minecraft 1.9 redstone capabilities. If you are playing with a different version of Minecraft, you may find some differences. For the latest information on a device or item, check the Minecraft Wikipedia, at Minecraft.gamepedia.com.

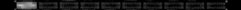

For a redstone contraption to work, there must be a source of power or redstone signal. Some power sources send power constantly, like redstone torches. Other sources only emit power when they are turned on, like a switch. Some, like buttons, may only send a redstone signal for a short period of time.

Power sources send power to themselves (the block space they are in) and also, usually, to the blocks they are attached to. Different power source items have slightly different rules about what blocks (or block spaces) they send power to.

Some power sources also power the blocks *next to* the block they are attached to. These include buttons, detector rails, levers, pressure plates, and tripwire hooks. Your main power sources will be redstone torches, redstone blocks, buttons, and levers.

Redstone Torches

A redstone torch provides power constantly, to itself and to the block above it. It will provide power to attached redstone dust, repeaters and comparators, and attached redstone devices like pistons. (The repeaters must be facing away from the torch, as this devices receives signals from the back. Comparators receive signals from the side or back.) A redstone torch doesn't provide power to the block it is placed on. In fact, if the block the redstone torch is on receives power from another block or source, the redstone torch will turn *off*.

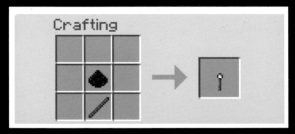

Redstone torch recipe.

Redstone Blocks

A redstone block is another power source that is always on. Unlike a torch though, it can't be turned off. It powers redstone dust, comparators, repeaters, and most redstone devices above, below, or around it, like doors or redstone lamps. The exception is a piston, which cannot be activated if the power source is directly in front of it.

Redstone block recipe.

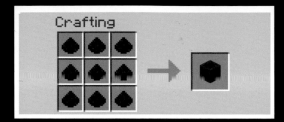

Levers

A lever provides a constant power source when it is turned on. When you place a lever, it is in the off position. It provides power to the block it is on, and any attached redstone dust or devices.

Lever recipe.

Buttons

Buttons can be made of either stone or wood, and they provide power only for a short time. A stone button will send power for 1 second, while a wood button will send power for 1.5 seconds. (One exception is if an arrow hits a wood button, the arrow will keep the button pressed until the arrow despawns or is picked up.) Buttons power the block they are on and any attached redstone dust or devices.

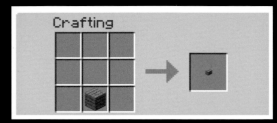

Wood button recipe.

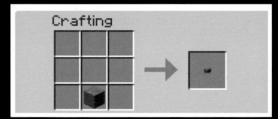

Stone button recipe.

Pressure Plates

Like buttons, pressure plates provide temporary power and are made of stone or wood. Stone or wood pressure plates provide power for 1 second, or for the time an item or entity is on it. Pressure plates are activated by players, mobs, or a minecart with a mob in it. Wooden plates can also be activated by arrows, fishing rod lures, any minecart, and any dropped items. A pressure plate powers the block beneath it, and any attached redstone dust or devices.

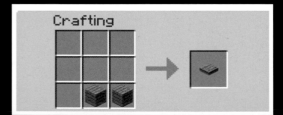

Wood pressure plate recipe.

Stone pressure plate recipe

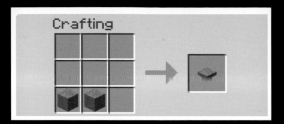

Weighted Pressure Plates

Weighted pressure plates are similar to regular pressure plates but are made of either gold or iron. They are different from regular pressure plates only in the strength of signal they produce. Their signal depends on the number of mobs or items on top of them. The light (gold) pressure plate gives out a signal strength equal to the number of mobs, up to 15. So 8 items on the plate will make it send out a signal for 8 blocks, and 16 will make it send out a signal of 15 blocks. The heavy (iron) plate needs many more mobs to give increased signal strength. It will only reach the full 15-block-long strength when more than 140 mobs are on it.

Weighted pressure plate (light) recipe.

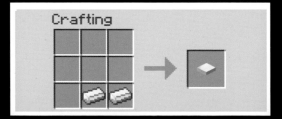

Weighted pressure plate (heavy) recipe.

Detector Rails

A detector rail provides a power signal when a minecart is on it. It will power any attached redstone dust and devices, as well as the block it is on. Detector rails are often used to switch the tracks a minecart is on. If a minecart with a chest or hopper is on it, the detector rail will send a signal strength that shows how full that container is.

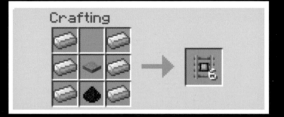

Detector rail recipe.

Tripwire Hooks

You can make a tripwire from two tripwire hooks connected with string. The two hooks power the blocks they are attached to when the string between them is stood on or walked over. They also provide power to attached redstone dust and devices. The two tripwire hooks can be up to 40 blocks apart.

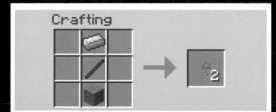

Tripwire hook recipe.

Trapped Chests

Trapped chests provide power when they are opened to attached redstone dust and devices, as well as the block they are placed on. The power sent to redstone dust or the block will be the same as the number of players opening the chest, with a maximum strength of 15. Unlike many devices, however, they won't provide power to a comparator. A comparator can still measure the signal strength of a trapped chest.

Trapped chest recipe.

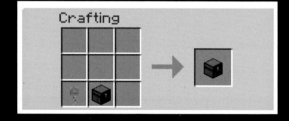

Daylight Sensors

Daylight sensors activate in the presence of sunlight. The amount of power they provide depends on the strength of the sunlight, so during dawn their signal strength will rise upwards from 1 to a maximum of 15 during full sunlight. During sunset, their power decreases until there is no sunlight left. You can also invert a daylight sensor by right-clicking it. An inverted sensor does the opposite—the amount of power it provides depends on how little sunlight there is. That means the strength will increase the darker it gets. Daylight sensors are great objects for making redstone contraptions that turn on and off at certain times of the day, like automatic street lighting.

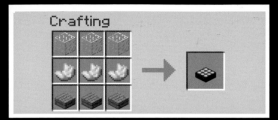

Daylight
sensor recipe.

Containers

Containers are items that can store things and have inventories. Brewing stands, chests, dispensers, droppers, furnaces, hoppers, and jukeboxes are all containers. They provide a power signal to a comparator. The strength of the signal depends on how full they are. A chest with 27 slots but only 3 items will send a weaker signal than a hopper with 5 slots and 3 items. How full they are also depends on the sizes of the stacks of the items they contain. A chest filled with eggs (which stack to 16) will send a stronger signal than a chest half filled with sticks (which stack to 64). Even though the second chest has more items, the first chest has used more of the potential space. One exception is the jukebox. The signal it sends out depends on which disc is in it; different discs have different strengths.

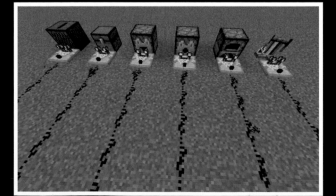

Containers
send signals to
comparators
showing how full
they are.

CHAPTER 2

REDSTONE DUST AND SIGNALS

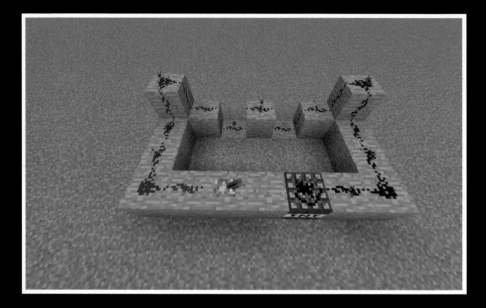

You can power devices by placing the power source right next to the device, but you will often want to separate the two. To do this, you use redstone dust, which carries the power from source to device. Redstone dust that is carrying power sparkles and emits particles. If it is unpowered, there are no particles.

Redstone dust has some traits that can make moving a signal a bit tricky.

Redstone Dust Signals Only Travel 15 Blocks

Every block that redstone dust travels, the signal strength it carries decreases. The highest strength is 15, and the maximum distance redstone dust can carry a signal by itself is 15 blocks. This means that if powered redstone dust runs for two blocks, its strength at the end of those two blocks is 13, because 15 (the maximum power) minus 2 (the power it lost) is 13. You can change the length a redstone signal travels by using a device called a redstone repeater.

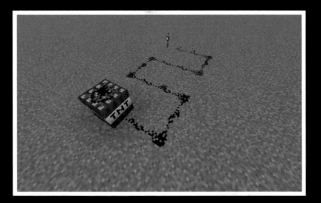

Redstone signal stops after 15 blocks.

Redstone Dust Can't Be Placed on All Blocks

You can't place redstone dust on most transparent blocks (blocks you can see through) like grass and glass, or stairs or slabs. However, you can put redstone on upside-down slabs, (slabs placed in the top half of a block space), on top of upside-down stairs, and on glowstone.

Redstone can't travel over bottom slabs or most transparent blocks. It can travel over upside-down (top half) slabs.

Redstone Dust Has to Be Placed Properly to Power a Device or Block

Redstone needs to point at a device or block in order to power it. If your trail of redstone dust travels by a device without pointing at it, it won't power the block. The exception to this is when you place just one single dot of redstone dust and it points nowhere. This can power blocks to all four sides.

This redstone dust powers only the dropper on the left.

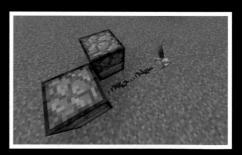

This single dot of redstone dust is "directionless," because it's not pointing anywhere. It can transmit power to all sides, so all three of these droppers are powered.

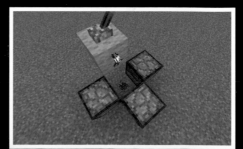

Redstone Weakly Powers Blocks

Redstone powers the blocks it is on and points to when it is active and lit up. It is said to do this weakly, because the blocks that are powered this way don't have enough power to turn on attached redstone dust, but they do have enough power to activate repeaters, comparators, and other redstone devices.

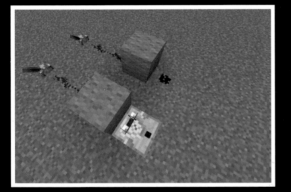

Here, redstone dust sends the same power to two blocks. It is enough power to turn on an attached comparator (bottom) but not enough to turn on redstone (top).

Redstone Dust Can Only Travel 1 Block Vertically

To move redstone dust vertically more than one block, you need to use a staircase, so that it travels one block over for each block it rises. You can also use glowstone or upside-down slabs in an alternating pattern. Because these two blocks are both seen as transparent, they don't cut off the signal at the block edges where they touch.

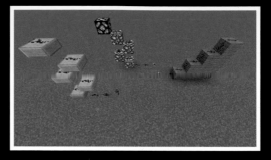

Three ways of moving a signal up: Upside-down slabs (left), glowstone (middle), and a staircase (right).

A fourth alternative is to use redstone torches in an alternate pattern. Because these turn the signal off and then on, you have to be careful that the final torch is on to maintain the signal.

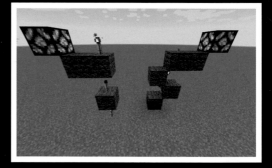

You can also alternate torches to move a signal up.

These methods only work for moving a signal up. To move a signal down, you will have to use a staircase or create a special contraption. You can make a spiral staircase that takes up less space.

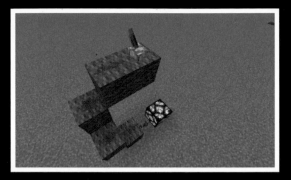

A spiral staircase can move signals down (and up) in a small space.

Changing the Redstone Signal

There are two devices you can use to change the power of the signal traveling along redstone dust. These are the repeater and the comparator, and they are very important parts of many redstone contraptions.

Redstone Repeaters

The redstone repeater takes a redstone signal pointed to its back and refreshes it to the full 15 power level. This allows you to carry a signal farther than 15 blocks. At the fifteenth block or earlier, before the redstone fizzles out, place a repeater pointing in the direction the signal is moving. There's an arrow on the repeater that shows you which way it is pointing. There are also two mini-torches that light up when the repeater is powered.

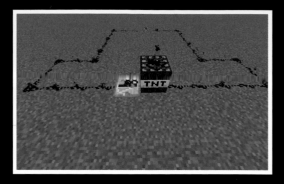

The signal on the right is too long to reach the TNT. On the left, a repeater makes it happen.

Repeaters also can delay a signal. Traveling through a repeater delays the signal by 1 redstone tick. You can change this to a delay of 2, 3, or 4 ticks by right-clicking the repeater. When you do this, the back torch changes position to show the change in delay.

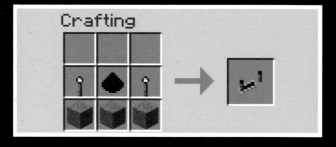

Repeater recipe.

What's a Redstone Tick?

A redstone tick lasts about one tenth of a second, and redstone contraptions measure and react to each other based on this unit of time. A redstone tick is twice the length of a game tick, which lasts one twentieth of a second. Game ticks are used in programming the game to measure and time events, like when plants grow.

Redstone Comparators

A comparator is a bit like a repeater, and it looks very similar, except it has three mini-torches on it instead of two. Like a repeater, it has an arrow on it that shows the direction it is pointing. It takes a signal coming in from the back and compares it to a signal coming in at its side. The comparator outputs a signal that is the same strength as the back signal, *unless* there is a side signal that has greater strength. (There can be two side signals, left and right.) Then the comparator will produce no signal. This is called comparison mode.

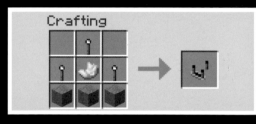

Redstone comparator recipe.

The front torch of this comparator is unlit, so you know it is in compare mode. The side signal is stronger (it's closer) than the back, so the comparator sends no signal out its front.

You can also put the comparator into subtract mode. To do this, right-click the comparator, and the front torch will light up. In subtract mode, the comparator will take the back signal strength, and subtract the greatest of any side signal. The signal it puts out is equal to the result. So if the strongest side signal is level 4, and the back signal is level 15, it will output a signal of level 11.

The comparator is in subtract mode here—the front torch is on. It subtracts the side signal (0) from the back signal (12), for an output signal strength 3. Enough strength to set off that TNT.

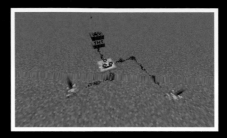

Comparators can also measure containers and produce a signal whose strength depends on how full the container is. You can read more about this in chapter 1. No signal is produced when the container is empty, and a full strength signal is produced when the container is completely full. Comparators can also measure a cake (how many slices it has), item frames (what position the item is rotated to), and cauldrons (how much water they have).

The cake on the left is whole with its full 7 slices intact. Each slice has a value of 2 (for cake fullness sensing). Its comparator sends out the maximum uneaten cake power strength of 14. The cake on the right has a slice taken from it. So its comparator sends out a cake power signal that is only 12 blocks strong.

CHAPTER 3

REDSTONE DEVICES

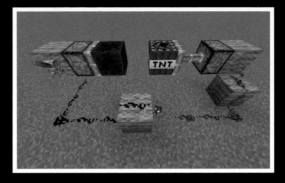

R edstone devices are items that do something when you give them a redstone signal. Dispensers and droppers eject items, trapdoors open, and pistons extend their arms.

Dispensers

Dispensers and droppers look like they have faces. The dispenser looks surprised!

When you power a dispenser, it ejects one item, chosen randomly from its inventory. It has a 9-slot inventory that you access by right-clicking it.

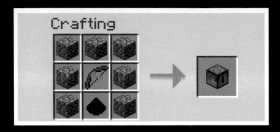

Dispenser recipe.

The dispenser ejects most items in the same way you drop items with the Q key (or another key assigned to the Drop Item command). It drops items into the one block in front of it. However, with some items, it will place and/or activate the item. These special interactions include:

- Armor—Puts armor on a player if the player is within 1 block and has that armor slot empty

- Arrows—Fired in the direction the dispenser is facing

- Boats—Places boats in water

- Bonemeal—Applies bonemeal to a crop

- Bucket—Removes a lava or water source

- Fire Charge—Explodes with fireballs toward a target

- Fireworks—Places and activates fireworks

- Flint and steel—Sets fire to the block in front

- Lava—Places a lava source

- Minecarts—Places minecarts on a rail (if rail is there)

- Mob Heads—Places pumpkins or mob heads on players, mobs, and stands. Completes golems and withers when the appropriate head is dispensed

- Projectiles—Throws or fires a projectile (these include arrows, eggs, snowballs, and splash potions)

- TNT—Places and activates TNT

- Water—Places a water source

When a dispenser ejects any item other than a projectile, it clicks and releases smoke particles. When you place a dispenser, it will always face toward you. If you need it to face a particular direction, first stand in that direction.

Doors

These include all types of doors, fence gates, and trapdoors. Doors open when you give them a redstone signal and close when the signal stops.

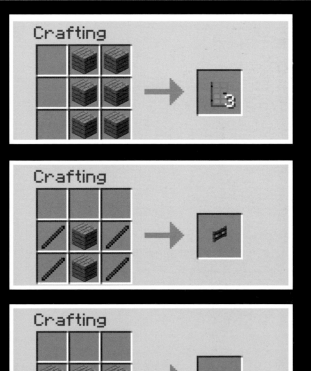

Oak door recipe.

Oak fence gate recipe.

Wood trapdoor recipe.

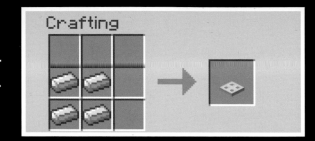

Iron trapdoor recipe.

Droppers

A dropper is almost identical to a dispenser. It has a 9-slot inventory and it ejects items through its front, just like a dispenser. There are two main differences. First, the dropper never activates, places, or fires items. Second, it can place items in containers placed in front of it. When you power a dropper, it ejects 1 item chosen randomly from its inventory. Droppers can also eject items through a block of glass.

A dropper looks the same as a dispenser except for its smile!

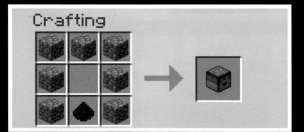

Dropper recipe.

A hopper moves items around. It will suck in any items that you drop into the one block of air above it. A hopper will also automatically take items from a chest or container placed directly above it. It transfers items to any container that its output tube (at the bottom) points to.

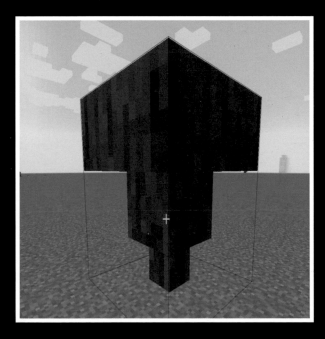

Hoppers transfer items to other containers.

Hoppers can remove and add items to: chests, furnaces, dispensers, droppers, brewing stands, other hoppers, and minecarts with chests and hoppers. Unlike many redstone devices, if a hopper *receives* redstone power, it will stop transferring items. A hopper has an inventory with only 5 slots.

Hopper recipe.

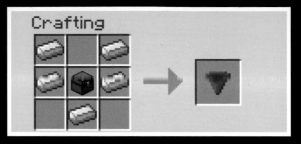

You will need to press shift when you right-click to place a hopper on top of some objects, like chests. If you want a hopper to point to a chest or another item sideways (rather than from above), shift-right-click the side of the chest or item with the hopper in your hand.

Shift-right-click on a chest or container with the hopper to make the hopper's output tube point to that chest.

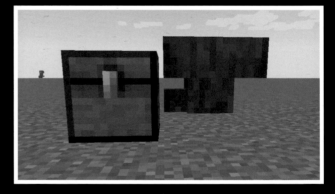

More about Hoppers:

- Hoppers transfer items one at a time, starting with the leftmost slot in an inventory.

- You can make a hopper pipe of several hoppers in a chain, one pointing to the next.

- Hoppers can only work with chests that can be opened. If your cat is sitting on a chest, the hopper won't pull or push items to it. Also, hoppers don't work with Ender chests.

- When a hopper is above a brewing stand, it only transfers items to the stand's top ingredient slot. When it is pointed to the side of the stand, it only transfers to the potion slots. When it is below the stand, it only takes from the potion slots.

- When a hopper is above a furnace, it transfers items only to the ingredient slot. When it points to the furnace side, it only transfers fuel items. When it is beneath the furnace, it only takes smelted items.

Minecart Rails

Two types of minecart rails are devices. If you power an activator rail, it will activate certain types of minecarts that run over it. Regular minecarts will eject any mobs or players in them. Hopper minecarts will *stop* picking up items. TNT minecarts will set off the TNT.

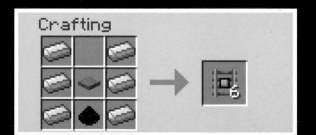

Detector rail recipe.

Powered rails respond to a redstone signal by speeding up a minecart passing over them. They're used to keep minecarts going fast and to propel them uphill.

Powered rail recipe.

Pistons and Sticky Pistons

When you power a piston or a sticky piston block, it uses a wooden arm to extend its front side, called its head, out one block. Any block that was in front of it is pushed as well. When the power signal is removed, the piston retracts. With a regular piston, the block it pushed remains where it is. With a sticky piston, the block it pushed retreats with the head.

Piston recipe.

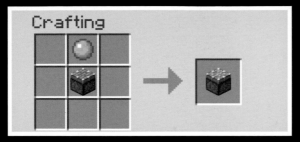

Sticky piston recipe.

Either type of piston can move up to 12 blocks in front of it. However, when a sticky piston retracts, it only pulls back the one block it touches. The regular piston pulls back no blocks.

When you place a piston, its head faces toward you. To get it to face a particular direction, you need to move to the location you want it to face.

There are some blocks a piston can't move. These include bedrock, obsidian, portal blocks, and anvils. Pistons also cannot move blocks that can perform special actions. These include beds, brewing stands, chests, dispensers, droppers, hoppers, furnaces, and chests. Also, some blocks will turn into their drops when a piston pushes them: These include cacti, doors, dragon eggs, flowers, melons, pumpkins, sugar cane, and torches.

Slime blocks react in a special way with pistons. You can push *and* pull up to 12 total connected slime blocks (and regular blocks that are connected to a slime block). All these blocks *don't* have to be directly in front of the piston's head. A sticky piston will also move regular blocks not connected directly to a slime block as long as the total blocks to move add up to 12 or less. It won't pull these back, however.

A sticky piston can move blocks that aren't directly in front of it, as long as they are connected by slime (and don't number more than 12).

Redstone Lamps

A redstone lamp is like a glowstone lamp and is made with glowstone. It will only turn on when it gets a redstone power signal. They are often used to make street lighting (hooked up with an inverted daylight sensor) as well as home and mob trap lighting.

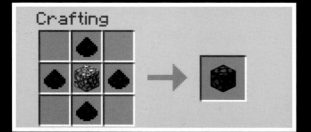

Redstone lamp recipe.

There are several ways to set off TNT. It will go off if it's touched by fire or lava or the explosion of another TNT. You can ignite TNT with a flint and steel or shoot it with a fire charge or a bow enchanted with Flame I. You can also set it off with redstone. A redstone signal will activate it, and a dispenser can place and activate TNT in its inventory.

TNT recipe.

CHAPTER 4

AUTO SMELTER

This small automatic smelter is very easy to make and quite helpful in a survival world. Drop smeltable items and fuel in the top two chests, and they'll all end up smelted in the bottom.

What You Need:

3 chests

3 hoppers

1 furnace

*I've also used additional blocks—red brick, red brick stairs, and stone bricks—to decorate this build.

1. Dig a hole one wide and 2 long. At the front of the hole, place your chest.

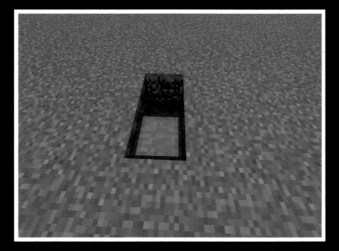

2. In the hole behind the chest, place a hopper that is pointing toward the chest. (To do so, press shift and right-click the back of the chest while you hold the hopper.)

3. Place a furnace on top of the hopper. (To do this, shift-right-click the hopper with the furnace in your hand.)

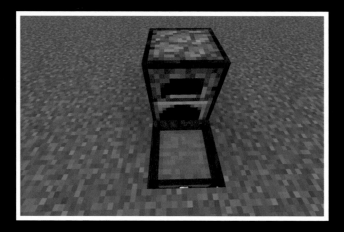

4. Place a hopper pointing into the side of the chest, and another above the chest. The side hopper will place coal or other fuel into the fuel slot, and the upper hopper will place smeltable items into the furnace's top slot.

5. Place two chests, one above each hopper you placed in step 4. The hoppers below will automatically remove items from the chest above them. You are done! You can pretty the contraption up, as I did below, or just start using it. You can also easily modify this to use double chests. And since there's no redstone dust or repeaters and such, an accidental water spill won't destroy this contraption.

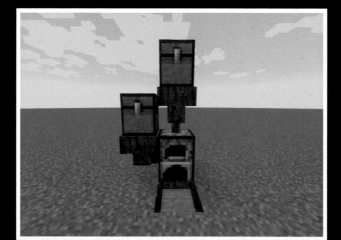

CHAPTER 5

TNT CANNON

What's more fun than blowing stuff up with TNT? Blowing stuff up with a TNT cannon! This is a classic Minecraft cannon, with some extra blocks to make it look a bit more like an actual old-timey weapon.

WARNING

When you are working with TNT and redstone, always wait till the very end before you place the TNT. It is very easy to set off TNT accidentally when you are playing around with redstone connected to it!

What You Need:

26 spruce wood planks

8 (4x2) spruce wood steps

2 spruce wood fences

3 stone blocks

1 stone button

56 coal blocks

18 redstone dust

4 repeaters

7 TNT (for each cannon shot!)

1 bucket of water

1. Build your cannon's base, or carriage, out of 18 spruce wood planks. First, place two rows of 3 planks. On top of this bottom level, place three rows of 3 planks. This level should be offset from the bottom level by 1 block. Above the middle row of this level, build just one row of 3 planks.

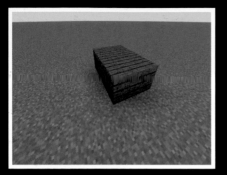
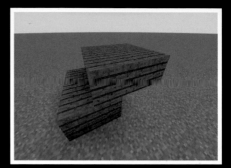

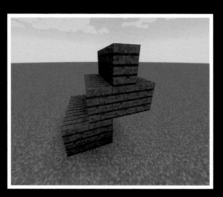

2. Add the bottom of the cannon. Make a 3-block wide and 9-block long rectangle of coal blocks.

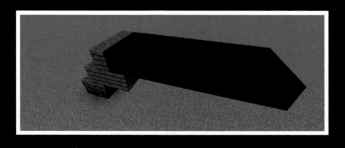

3. Add the sides, front, and back of the cannon. Add a 1-block coal block row to the two sides of the cannon, and 1 block at either end, between the two long rows.

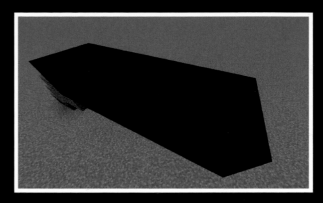

4. Add the axle for the wheels. Underneath the cannon, next to the spruce wood base, place one row, 3 blocks long, of stone blocks.

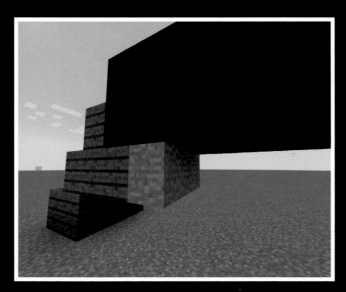

5. Increase the size of the cannon's base. Add a 2-block wide, 3-block long row of coal blocks next to the axle, to make the cannon's base, or breech, look a little bigger than the muzzle of the cannon.

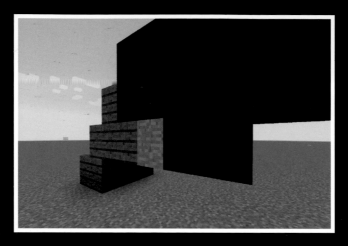

6. On each end of the axle, build out large wheels for the carriage. First, build a cross shape, with a space in the center, of spruce wood blocks.

7. Add spruce wood stairs to round out the wheels. Add a spruce wood fence in the center of each wheel.

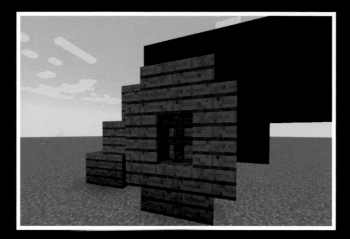

8. At the back, or breech, of the cannon, place 1 coal block, 1 block in from the sides and 1 block above.

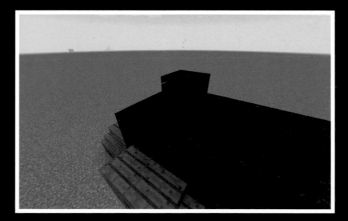

9. Right underneath the block you placed in step 8, use your water bucket to place a water source block. The water should run 8 blocks, from here just to the front of the cannon.

10. On one side of the cannon, place 8 redstone dust in a line, starting from the backmost block. At the cannon's muzzle, there should be 1 block without redstone.

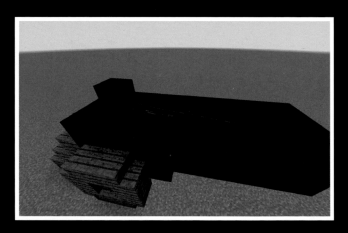

11. On the other side of the cannon, starting from the back-most block, place a line of 2 redstone dust, followed by 4 repeaters that point toward the muzzle. Right-click each of the repeaters 3 times to give them each the maximum 4-tick delay.

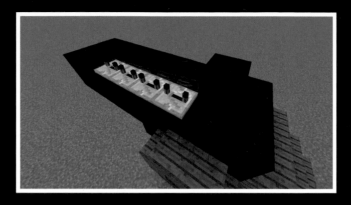

12. We're now going to continue this side's redstone signal with redstone dust, but also raise it up 1 block. This way the signal can reach the TNT that we'll be placing in the muzzle. Add 2 coal blocks to the very end of the side we are working on. Use 3 redstone dust to run the signal from the repeaters to the muzzle.

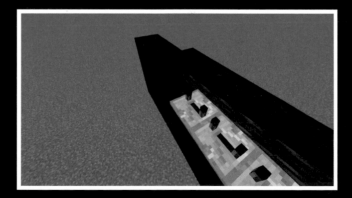

13. Place 1 redstone dust at the back of the cannon to join the two sides of dust. Place another 4 redstone dust to bring the redstone signal down to one side of the carriage.

14. On the same side of the carriage, place the button you'll use to set the cannon off.

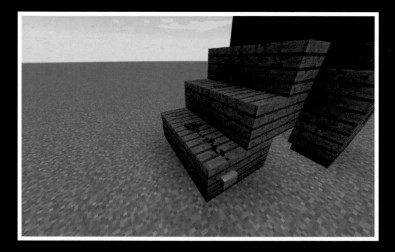

15. Place 1 block of TNT at the very end of the cannon at the muzzle, on top of the last coal block. This is the TNT that will be burst from the cannon.

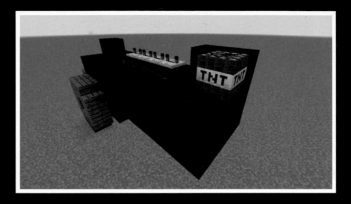

16. Place 6 TNT in the center water channel. (The water will look like it's disappearing; that is fine.) Be careful not to place TNT under the raised block at the back of the cannon, where you placed the water source. If you do, the water will disappear, and you'll need to replace it. The raised block is there to help remind you!

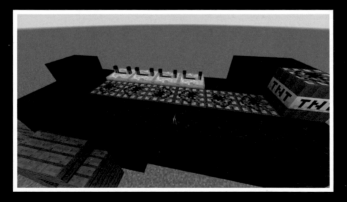

17. Press the button and stand back!! Enjoy watching the first 6 TNT build up power to blast the last one off before it explodes itself.

How Does It Work?

When you press the button, the redstone signal is carried on one side of the cannon to all six of the TNT in the water channel. The water will prevent the TNT from causing damage to any blocks, but it will set off and propel the TNT on the very end. On the other side of the cannon, the signal travels to the seventh TNT. It is delayed by the repeaters so that it doesn't explode before the six TNT in the water. It will explode after it has been hurled from the cannon. Sometimes it may go a little farther than other times, and sometimes it can explode in the air.

CHAPTER 6

SUPERFAST MINI FARM

This is the smallest farm you can have—it's only one block of dirt! But it can get you a stack of wheat, carrots, or potatoes in a hurry, if you have the bonemeal. In fact, because it relies on bonemeal, you may want to place this near your skeleton farm!

What You Need:

1 sticky piston

3 dispensers

3 repeaters

1 stone pressure plate

2 redstone torches

11 redstone dust

1 bucket of water

Lots of bonemeal

2–3 crop starters (grass seeds, carrots, or potatoes)

2+ building blocks (I've used 1 light blue wool and 1 orange wool in the contraption. For the décor I've used cobble, stone brick, spruce wood planks, slabs of these three, plus spruce wood, glowstone, and cobble stairs.)

1. Dig a 1x1 hole 3 blocks deep. At the bottom, place a sticky piston facing up. On top of the sticky piston, place a block of dirt. This will be the single block of dirt you farm on! (The piston will extend later on to make the dirt flush with the ground.)

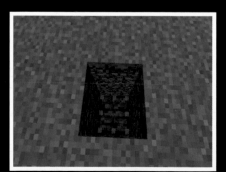 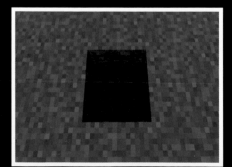

2. Replace the block of dirt in front of the hole with a block of your choice (I've used light blue wool), and on top of that place a stone pressure plate. This will be what you stand on when you are farming. The pressure plate will activate the contraption.

3. Around the other three sides of the hole, place dispensers facing inward. These will place three bonemeal on your farm to make your crops grow really fast.

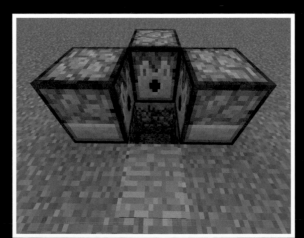

4. Dig out the sides and front around the light blue wool, in a U-shape. This trench should be 2 blocks deep. Also dig out the 1 block of dirt beneath the light blue wool.

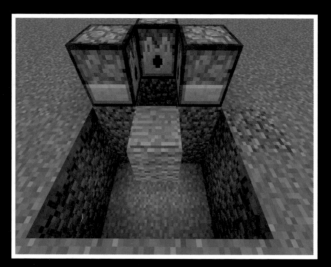

5. At the bottom of the trench, and to the right of the light blue wool, place another block. I've used orange wool here.

6. Now we're going to make a timing mechanism, or clock, that we'll use later to move our single block of dirt up and down. First, place a repeater pointing to the orange wool. Place a redstone torch on the front side of the orange wool.

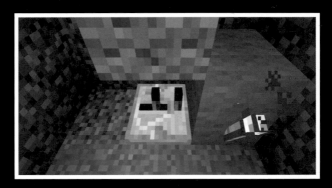

7. Connect the redstone torch to the back of the repeater with 3 redstone dust. The clock should start flashing on and off! Your clock should also sizzle out after a few rounds. This is called burn out and it happens to torches when the timing is too fast for them to keep up. To slow the pulse down, right-click the repeater once to give it a 2-tick delay. After a few moments, the torch will relight and the clock will start up again.

8. Now we are going to connect the clock to the pressure plate above. Place a redstone torch on the front of the light blue wool. This powers the redstone trail below it, turning off the torch on the orange wool. Now, when you step on the pressure plate, the torch beneath it will turn off. This will let the clock start pulsing again.

9. Next connect the clock to the sticky piston. Dig out the block that is two blocks beneath the left dispenser and place one redstone dust there. This powers on the piston, which extends and pushes the dirt block up.

10. Now we can connect the clock to the dispensers. On the center and right dispensers, place 2 repeaters pointing into them as shown. The repeaters help the redstone dust point in the right direction at the dispensers.

11. Dig out a trench, on the right of the contraption, to carry the redstone trail up from the clock to the two repeaters you have just placed. You'll need 6 redstone dust for this trail.

12. The third dispenser can be connected by placing 1 redstone dust to its side.

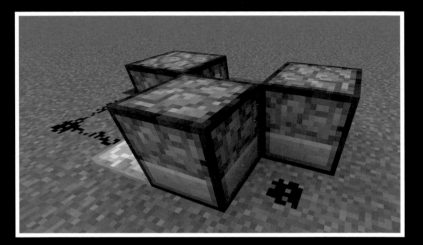

13. Now dig a hole behind the left dispenser and place your water in it. This will help keep the farm hydrated.

14. We're ready to test the farm. Add lots of bonemeal to the three dispensers, and hoe the dirt block between them so that it is ready for planting. To get your farm to start, stand on the pressure plate. With your wheat seeds (or carrots or potatoes) in your hand, right-click (and keep the right-click pressed) on the soil as it moves up and down. The dispensers will dispense bonemeal quickly. (The dispensers only place bonemeal if there is a crop before them.) As soon as your crop is mature it will pop off the dirt and into you!

NOTE: The pressure plate only gives out a signal when you are standing on it. If you replace it with a lever, you can turn your mechanism on and off so you can walk around it. Of course, it won't be planting or bonemealing crops, but you can look around to see the redstone flashing and the piston moving.

15. Now you can add any design touches you want. Here, I've covered up the redstone with cobble, stone brick, and spruce wood, and added spruce and glowstone columns.

I also added stairs up to the platform and down to the farming pressure plate. It might be a good idea to also add chests to hold bonemeal, hoes, seeds, and crops.

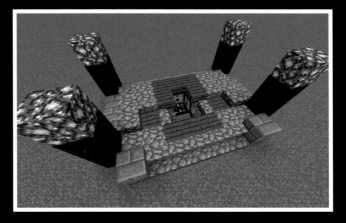

NOTE: When you decorate around your contraptions, be careful to leave space above the redstone dust. When redstone is being trailed up a block in a staircase fashion, the vertical trail going up (on the side of the block) also needs a block of space above it. It is easy to forget and cover this up, and stop the redstone pulse from traveling.

CHAPTER 7

COMBINATION LOCK

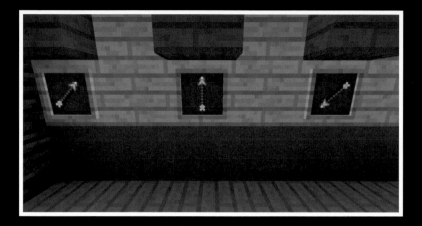

This combination lock on your door will keep strangers away from your precious goods! It uses three numbers, but you can easily expand it to use four, five, or more numbers, as you will see. This lock is best for an area that you will only open temporarily while you are there, like a special storage area.

The lock is based on the way that comparators behave with item frames. You've probably already seen that an item in an item frame can be rotated and goes through eight positions. A comparator can produce a signal based on that position. The item frame must be placed on a block behind the comparator for this to work. When there is no item in the frame, the comparator produces no signal. When you place an item in, and the item is straight up and down (or, the same way its icon appears in the Minecraft inventory), the comparator makes a signal strength of 1. Each time the item is rotated, the comparator increases the signal strength by one, up to the last position before it returns to normal, 8.

The arrow in this item frame is in the same position as the arrow icon you see in your inventory. Because it is in the default position, an attached comparator will send the default signal strength of 1.

Before creating your combination lock, decide what your three-number combination number will be. Each number must be between 1 and 8. The number of blocks and redstone you use will depend on your combination, as you will see. For this tutorial, we're using the combination number 3-8-5. Once you work through this project, you will see how you can easily change it to use your own secret number.

What You Need:

64+ blocks of your choice (I've used 33 birch blocks, 3 lime green wool, 27 yellow wool, and 1 magenta wool.)

1 iron door

3 item frames

3 arrows

3 comparators

4 redstone torches

4 repeaters

60+ redstone dust

1. Build a wall that is 3 blocks high and 11 blocks long using blocks of your choice. (I've used birch wood blocks.) Leave a 2-block space for a door on the right, 1 block in from the right side. This is the wall your lock and door will be on.

2. Place the iron door in the space you've left, and place 3 item frames 1 block up from the bottom of the wall, and spaced 1 block apart from each other, as shown. There should be 3 blocks between the rightmost item frame and the door. (The recipe for an item frame is 1 leather surrounded by 8 sticks.)

3. In each item frame, place an arrow. It should be pointing diagonally to the upper left, just as the arrow in your Minecraft inventory looks. This is position 1.

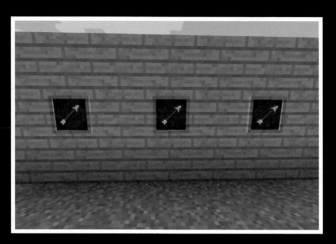

NOTE: For the item frame, you can choose any item that will clearly show what position it is in. This will be any item that isn't vertically symmetrical. Its top and bottom should be different, like an arrow, a sword, or a feather. If you use something that looks very much the same when it is rotated, like a snowball, it will be difficult to tell what position it is in.

4. Rotate each arrow to the position that shows what number it is. We are using the numbers 3 – 8 – 5 for the lock, so click the leftmost item frame 2 times to move the arrow to the 3 position. Click the middle item frame 7 times, and click the right frame 4 times.

5. Behind the wall, place 3 blocks on the ground, exactly opposite the item frames. I've used lime green wool. On top of these, place 3 comparators facing away from the item frames. Because the comparators are already detecting the item frames, they will light up.

6. Now let's test the signal strength of each comparator. Just above and in front of each comparator, place a row of 9 blocks (I've used yellow wool), for a total of 3 rows. On top of each of

these yellow wool blocks place redstone dust. Now look at how far the redstone signal travels on each. The comparator behind the leftmost item frame at position 3 should have 3 blocks of dust lit up. The second comparator should send the signal 8 blocks, and the third or rightmost should send the signal only 5 blocks. (If you have different results, check the position of the item in the item frame.)

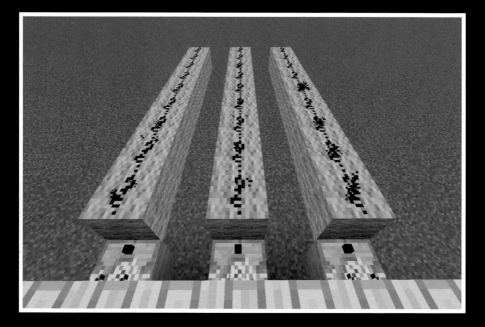

7. Now remove all of the blocks on these rows that are not carrying signal, leaving just the redstone and yellow wool blocks that are lit up. The left row will be 3 blocks long, the middle will be 8 blocks long, and the right will be 5 blocks long.

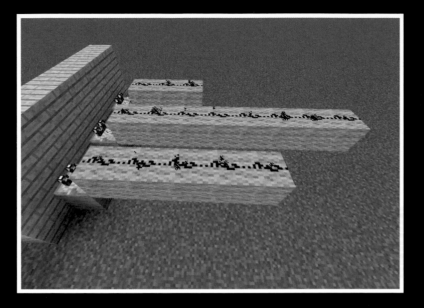

8. On the very end of all 3 rows, place a redstone torch as shown. Notice that the signal traveling from the comparator turns these torches off.

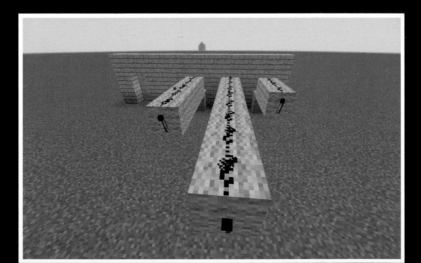

9. Beneath each row, add redstone dust that reaches from the green wool holding the comparator to the block right below the torch at the end.

10. At the end of each line of redstone you just placed, add a repeater facing away from the wall.

11. At the end of the longest row of yellow blocks add 1 red-stone dust. Add enough redstone dust at the end of the other 2 rows so that they reach the same length as the first, as shown.

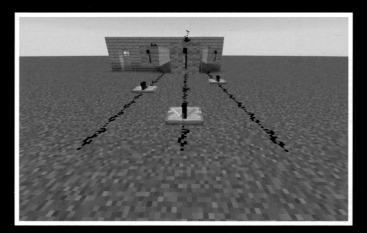

12. Use 2 redstone dust to connect the 3 lines at their ends.

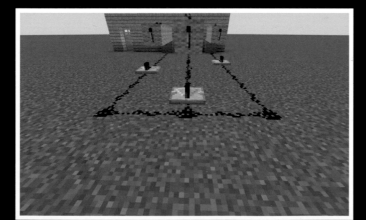

13. At the end of the redstone line nearest the door, place 3 redstone dust to bring the signal out and then change direction toward the door, as shown.

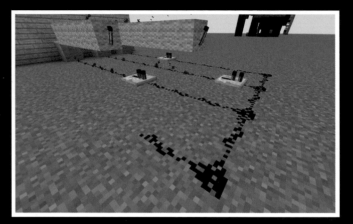

14. Place a repeater facing toward the door at the end of the line you just created.

15. Run redstone dust from the repeater all the way back to the wall. Stop just 1 block before you reach the wall.

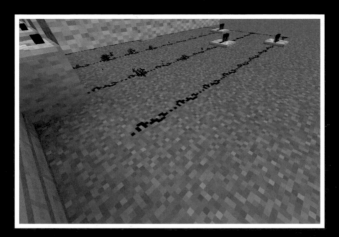

16. At the wall, on the same side as your redstone, break the 2 blocks next to the door and the 2 blocks in front of this, as shown.

17. Now use 3 redstone dust to connect the trail to the block beside the door, as shown.

18. At the moment, the redstone is working the *opposite* to the way we want it. The door will remain closed whenever the combination is right. It will open whenever the combination is wrong. Test this out by changing the position of an arrow in one of the item frames. To fix this, we change the signal to be the opposite of what it is now. First, break 2 of the redstone dust in the last trail that leads to the door.

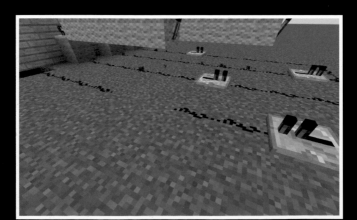

19. On the side closest to the last repeater, place 1 block. I've used magenta wool.

20. On the front side of the block you just placed, facing the wall, place a redstone torch. The redstone torch will be turned off from any signal coming to the block it is on. If there is no signal, it will send its own signal to the door. Congratulations! You are done with the redstone! Go test your lock, changing the item frames to the right positions and the wrong positions.

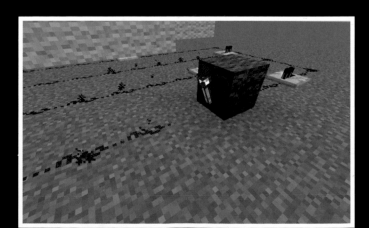

21. Now you can add any design touches you want. Here, I've created a storage building. I closed off the redstone section and added a storage room with lots of chests, furnaces, and crafting tables. I've used jungle wood, acacia and birch wood planks, slabs, and stairs, orange-stained clay, glowstone, and birch wood fence.

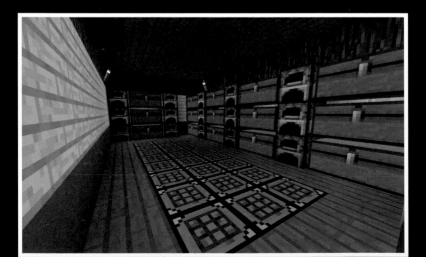

How to Customize the Lock

You can change this lock so that it uses your own private number. You will need to change the length of each row of redstone behind the item frame to match the numbers you choose. To do this, just follow steps 4 through 12 again to determine how long the row needs to be and to hook it up to the rest of the rows. You can also add more numbers, by copying and adding the same pattern of item frame, comparator, redstone dust, and repeaters to this setup.

How It Works

Each item frame–comparator combination sends out a signal whose length in blocks is the same as the item's position. If the item frame arrow is in the wrong position, the comparator will send out a signal that is either too long or too short. If the signal is too long, the redstone dust beneath the yellow wool will reach the repeater, and turn the redstone signal to the final repeater on. (The final repeater is there to make sure none of the redstone signals fizzle out because the lines of dust are too long.) If the signal is too short, the redstone dust will not reach either the top torch or the bottom repeater. However, this lets the redstone torch turn back on. The torch then powers the redstone signal reaching the final repeater before the door. If any signal comes through to the final repeater, the repeater will send along the signal to the torch and turn it off. The torch off means that no signal to open the door will reach the door. Only when *all* of the three possible signals from the comparators are *off* will a redstone signal, from the very last redstone torch, reach the door and open it.

CHAPTER 8

AUTOMATIC STORAGE SYSTEM

nce you've been mining for a while in Minecraft, you start getting lots of stuff. Lots of coal, lots of redstone, lapis, gold, iron, and hopefully diamonds! You can use a redstone contraption to help sort all your loot out when you make it back home. This sorting and storage system will let you put everything into a single chest. Then it will sort all these items and place them into separate chests for you! Best of all, you can easily expand it later with more chests to hold more stuff.

What You Need:

8 single chests

6 single trapped chests

39 blocks of your choice (I've used 12 birch wood planks, 3 red wool, 6 light blue wool, 6 lime green wool, 6 white wool, and 6 yellow wool.) On the finished contraption, I've used additional blocks for decoration (birch wood stairs, planks, and slabs and spruce wood).

6 comparators

6 repeaters

37 hoppers

12 redstone dust

6 redstone torches

6 item frames (or, to make these, 48 sticks and 6 leather)

12 samples of storage items (For each type of item you want to store, you will need 2 blocks or pieces of that item, 1 for the item frame and 1 for a hopper that helps sort items. For this example system, you'll need 2 diamonds, 2 gold ingots, 2 iron ingots, 2 coal ore, 2 lapis ore, and 2 redstone dust.)

126 buffer items to use in the filtering system (You will need to choose an item that you don't want to store in your system AND that can stack to 64. I've used 126 dandelions, but you could use 126 jungle saplings or 126 cobble, for example.)

1. Create a 2-block wide by 6-block long platform for your chests. I've used birch wood planks, because they match the frames on item frames. One long side will be the front of your storage system.

2. Place 2 single chests at one end of the platform to create 1 double chest.

3. In front of the double chest, place 2 trapped chests to make a double trapped chest. Trapped chests are like regular chests, except they produce a redstone signal when they are opened. But they have another handy trait that we are using them for. They can be placed right up against a regular chest. This means you can alternate placing regular chests and trapped chests to fit more chests in the same area.

4. Alternate placing double chests and trapped double chests on your base, until you have 6 double chests total on your base.

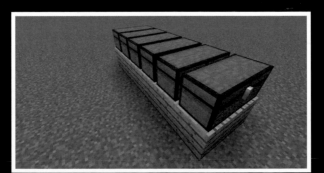

5. On the front of the platform, place an item frame below each chest. Right-click each item frame with the item you want to place in that chest. I've put in diamond, gold ingot, iron ingot, redstone, lapis lazuli, and coal. (You can craft an item frame with 1 leather surrounded by 8 sticks.)

Item frame recipe.

6. On the other side of the chests—the back side of the platform—place a row of 6 blocks (I've used lime green wool) 1 block away from the platform.

7. On the far side of each lime green wool, place a repeater facing into the wool.

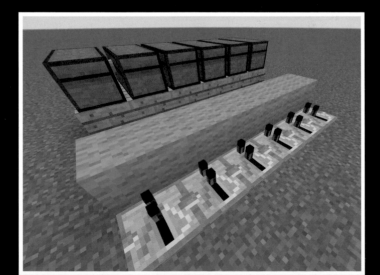

8. On the other side of each lime green wool, place a redstone torch.

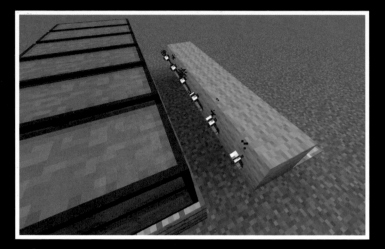

9. On top of the redstone torches, place a row of 6 hoppers. Each hopper should face into the chest next to it. You can make it do this by pressing shift as you right-click with the hopper.

10. Place a row of 6 blocks (I've used light blue wool) next to this bottom row of hoppers and above the row of lime green wool.

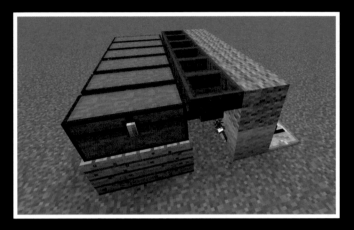

11. On top of the light blue wool, place a row of 6 comparators. Each comparator should be facing away from the chests and hoppers.

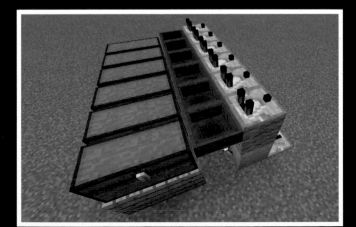

12. Above the bottom row of hoppers, place another row of 6 hoppers. Each hopper should point into the comparators. To do this, press shift as you right-click the back side of each comparator.

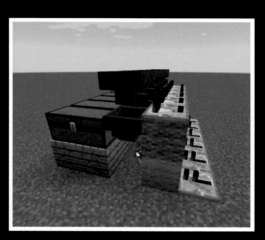

13. On the other side of the comparators, place a row of 6 blocks of your choice alongside the light blue wool. I've used yellow wool here. On top of each block, place 1 redstone dust.

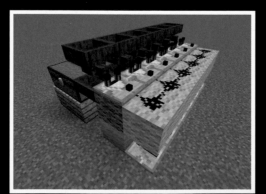

14. On the back side of the row of repeaters on the ground, place a row of 6 blocks of your choice. I've used white wool. On top of each block, place 1 redstone dust. (This will connect to the redstone on the yellow wool.)

15. In this storage system, items are placed in a chest on the left to be sorted into the 6 chests, and any items that overflow or don't match one of the 6 stored items will be collected by a chest on the right. Make a base for the overflow chest by placing a column of 3 blocks of your choice (I've used red wool) at the far right, to the right of the last redstone torch. On top, place 1 chest.

16. Above the second row of hoppers, place another row of 7 hoppers. The first hopper you place should point into the overflow chest. Each of the next hoppers should point into the last hopper you placed. The seventh and final hopper you place will collect items from your input chest.

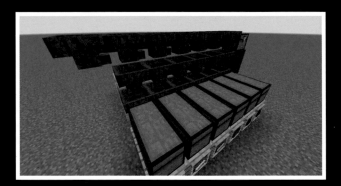

17. Place a chest above the last hopper you placed in step 16. This will be the input chest. Anything you put in this leftmost chest will travel down the line of top hoppers. It will be sorted into the chests below if it matches or end up in the overflow chest if it doesn't.

18. Now we need to configure the filtering system. The middle row of hoppers is used to filter and sort items. Each hopper will sort items for the chest it is next to. Right-click the hopper for the first chest. There are 5 inventory slots. Into the left inventory slot, place just 1 item of the type the chest is storing. I've put in 1 diamond, as this is my diamond chest. In the next 4 slots, place 21 items of your 126 buffer items. My buffer item is dandelions. I've put 1 dandelion in slots 2, 3, and 4, and 18 in slot 5, total 21 buffer items. It doesn't matter which slot they go into, as long as there are items in all of the four slots and they total 21.

19. Repeat this for the other 5 chests. Into the middle hopper for each chest, place 1 item of what the chest stores (the item you placed in the chest's item frame), plus 21 buffer items. Here are the hopper inventories from all six chests that store diamonds, gold ingots, iron ingots, lapis lazuli ore, redstone dust, and coal ore.

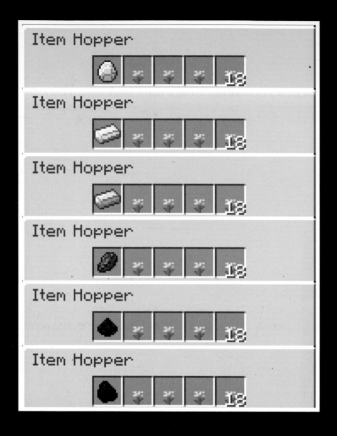

20. The contraption is finished! You can test the system by adding blocks to the input chest on the left. (The first time you run this, 1 item of each storage type will remain in the bottom hopper for its matching chest. This is fine, leave it in the bottom hopper.)

Blocks that don't match anything will move to the overflow chest. If blocks aren't ending up at the right chest, go over each construction step. Make sure the hoppers, comparators, and repeaters are pointing in the right direction, and that your buffer item isn't one of the ones you are storing.

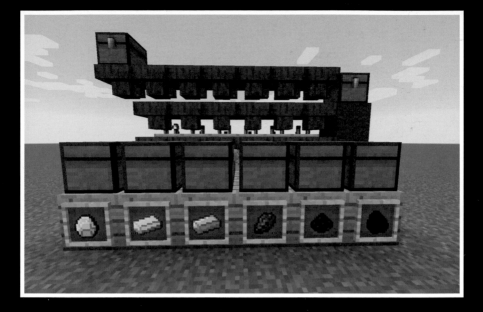

21. Finally, add any finishing design touches you want to cover the redstone up and make it easy to access all your chests. I've used birch wood planks, slabs, and stairs, and spruce wood to decorate this system.

Expanding your storage is very easy. For each chest you want to add, you will add 1 double chest (or trapped chest) and the blocks that go with it at the end of the line of chests and before the overflow chest. You'll need 1 item frame, 1 repeater, 1 comparator, 3 hoppers, 2 redstone dust, 1 redstone torch, and the blocks to hold these on, for each new chest. Don't forget to add the filter materials for each chest's middle hopper: 21 buffer items and 1 of the item the chest will hold.

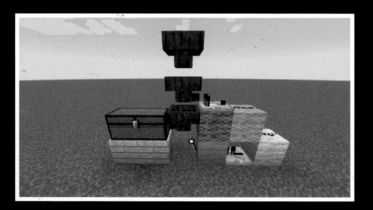

How It Works

An item you drop in the input chest travels down the top row of hoppers, in the direction the hoppers face. At each hopper, it checks below to see if it can fit into that hopper's inventory. Let's say the item is coal. At the diamond chest, it will see the middle hopper. This hopper's inventory slots all have either diamonds or the buffer item, dandelions. So nothing but diamonds or dandelions will fit into this hopper. The coal ore moves along until it reaches the hopper with 1 coal and 21 dandelions. Here it can fit! So the coal drops down into the middle hopper.

There are 23 items in this hopper now, and the hopper gives out a slightly stronger signal to the comparator it is facing. The output signal resulting from 22 items reached the 1 redstone dust in front of the comparator, while the signal from 23 items can reach the second redstone dust (1 block down). Now the signal can reach the repeater below, and turn the redstone torch off. This redstone torch was locking the very bottom hopper. With the redstone torch turned off now, the coal ore can pass through. Once the middle hopper has only 22 items again, it stops sending the signal that keeps the torch off, and the hopper stops sending items through to the chest.

The great thing about XP mob farms is that they let you kill mobs safely and in one spot, so you can gather all the XP and items they drop. It is helpful to "soften" the mobs up first by damaging them so that they only have one heart left. That way, you can just punch them once to get the XP—and you don't have to use up the durability of your weapons.

In this crusher, you'll use pistons to crush mobs, suffocating them to damage them, in a tiny 1x1 room. How you get the mobs there is up to you! One easy way is to use a water channel to push the mobs from a mob spawning room. (If you are not sure how to make a mob spawning room, see the notes at the end of this project!) This crusher will deal enough damage to mobs so that you can kill them afterwards with one hit.

What You Need:

2 sticky pistons

30 blocks of your choice (I've used colored wool to help show the steps, stone bricks, and glass.)

1 stone button

8 redstone dust

2 comparators

1 repeater

2 hoppers

3 redstone torches

*This doesn't include any blocks you use to gather and move your mobs into the grinder.

1. Plan your location. You will want to place the crushing room somewhere that you will have mobs you can push into it. Here I have a water channel that drops mobs down 2 blocks at the end, where the crushing room will be.

2. Place 2 pistons at the back of what will be the crushing room, one on top of the other. Leave a 1 block space in front of each for the blocks the pistons will push.

3. Add the 2 blocks you will be using to crush the mob, placing them against the pistons' fronts. These 2 blocks are the back wall of the room. I've used purple wool.

4. Catty-corner to the bottom purple wool, place 2 blocks of your choice. I've used yellow wool.

5. On top of the yellow wool, place 2 hoppers pointing at each other. To do this, you place 1 hopper first on the yellow wool. Then place a second hopper, pointing to the first, by shift-clicking the side of the first hopper. You will now need to break the first hopper. Replace it so that it points at the second hopper by shift-clicking the second hopper's side. The 2 hoppers' bottom funnels should point right at each other as shown in the picture.

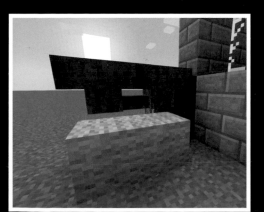

6. Behind the yellow wool and hoppers, place 2 blocks of your choice. (I've used lime green wool.) On top of these place 2 comparators pointing away from the hoppers. The arrows on the comparators should face the back of the contraption.

7. Next to the bottom piston, place 1 redstone dust.

8. Above the dust you just placed, and next to the top piston, place 2 blocks of your choice side by side. I've used cyan wool.

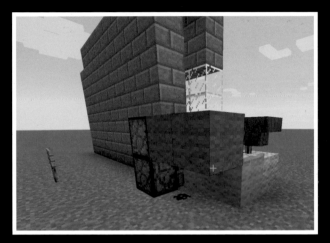

9. Place a redstone torch on the cyan wool that is farthest from the crushing room.

10. Next to the green wool and comparators, place another building block. (I've used orange wool.) On top of this, place a repeater that is facing the front of the contraption. The arrow should be pointing in the opposite direction as the comparators' arrows.

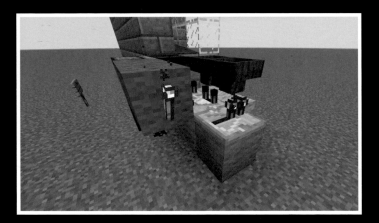

11. Place a block next to the outside hopper. I've used pink wool here. On top of this, place 1 redstone dust.

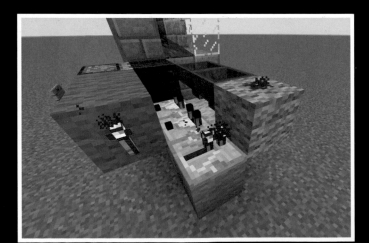

12. Now, on top of the outside hopper, place 3 blocks in an upside-down L shape. I've used light blue wool in the picture.

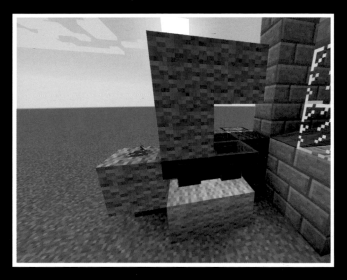

13. On the side of the top left block of light blue wool, place a redstone torch. Along the top place 2 redstone dust.

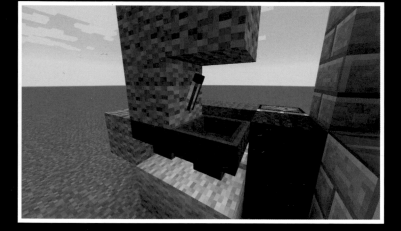

15. Now you will place the blocks and redstone dust that will connect to the button you use to turn the crusher on. Here I've used 4 red wool with 4 redstone dust on top of each. The last wool block has a stone button to use for starting the contraption.

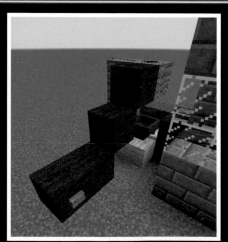

16. The hoppers you placed in step 5 are a type of timer. To make this work, place 12 blocks or items of your choice (I've used cobble) in the left, or outer, hopper. To do this, you can right-click the hopper to open its inventory, and drag the 12 blocks from your own inventory.

17. Congratulations! Except for finishing the crushing room, the contraption is done. Test it by pressing the button. The 2 pistons should extend for about 15 seconds, then retract. If they don't retract, go through all of the previous steps to make sure every item is placed correctly or pointing the right way.

18. Now all you have to do is finish the crushing room. The room will be just the 1x1 block of space that is at least 2 blocks high. If you are pushing or dropping your mobs in, it may need to be higher. The room I have is 4 blocks high so that mobs can come in from the water channel with a 2-block drop. Add blocks of your choice above the purple wool at the back wall. Add blocks to finish off the ceiling and left wall. I've used stone bricks and glass.

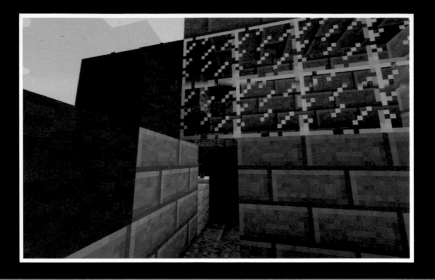

19. For the front wall of the crushing room use 2 half-slabs (placed as the top halves of blocks) as shown. This gives you space to swat at the crushed mobs. It also prevents any baby zombies from getting out and allows the XP orbs to easily flow to you at the bottom.

The contraption is set up so that the left hopper is powered. Powering a hopper prevents it from sending on items, like the cobblestone placed in it (although it can still receive items). Also notice that the comparator behind the left hopper is lit up, which means that it is receiving a signal from the left hopper. The hopper sends out a redstone signal when it contains items.

When you press the button, the redstone signal turns the left hopper off and the right hopper on. The left hopper starts sending the right hopper the 12 cobble. During this time, you can see that both comparators are lit up, because both hoppers have items. Also, the signal from the right comparator is hooked up to the pistons, so whenever the right comparator has items in it, the pistons are extended.

When the left hopper is empty, it stops sending its signal out through the comparator in the back, and this allows the farthest back torch to turn on. This sends a signal through the repeater. This then turns the front left redstone torch back on, and the front right redstone torch back off. And this powers on the left hopper and powers off the right hopper. The right hopper now sends the 12 items back to the left hopper. Once all 12 items are back to the left hopper, the right hopper's comparator signal turns off and the piston retracts.

More: The 12 items define how long the right comparator is on; it is the full length of time that it takes 12 items to move both to and from the right hopper. It takes 0.7 seconds to transfer 1 item, so transferring 12 items twice (12 x 2 x .7) is 16.8 seconds. If you are using this for mobs with more health than a skeleton, like Endermen or zombies with armor, you can lengthen the crushing time by adding more items to the left hopper. For armored-up zombies, however, you can also try dropping them a few more blocks before entering the crushing room so that they are already a bit damaged.

Mob Spawner Farm

If you have never built a mob XP farm before, the easiest is probably a spawner farm. To collect the mobs that spawn from a dungeon spawner, you first build an 8x8 room, at least 6 blocks high, around a spawner. The spawner should be in the center, in the air. Dig a 2-block deep channel on one side of the room (on the ninth block, so that you still have 8x8 floor space). One block of source water at one end of the channel will push mobs to the other end, where you can dig another 2-block deep hole or channel to keep pushing the mobs with water to where you want them.

In the 8x8 room itself, you need to push the mobs that spawn to the channel. Along the opposite wall from the channel, place water source blocks. Because water travels 8 blocks, this will push mobs right up to the edge of the channel, and they'll drop right in. Here's a picture:

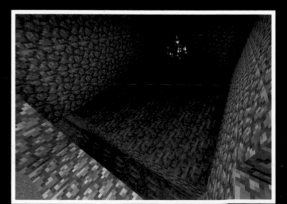

CHAPTER 10

VENDING MACHINE

You will need to choose 1 item as a payment for each item sold (for example, 1 diamond or 1 iron for each chicken, cake, or sword you are going to sell). However, hoppers are always enabled when they have no power going into them, which means that anything we put into the hopper will travel to the bottom chest. Therefore we first must disable the bottom hopper.

What You Need:

2 chests

4 hoppers

Colored wool (1 lime green, 1 blue, 2 magenta, 2 orange, 1 cyan)

3 redstone dust

2 repeaters

3 redstone torches

1 comparator

4 wooden swords

63 items of the payment type (for example, 63 iron ingots)

Stacks of the item you are selling (for example, roast chicken)

Additional building blocks for décor, as you like

1. Dig a hole 5 blocks wide by 4 blocks long that is 4 blocks deep. One of the long sides will be the front, where the vending machine will be.

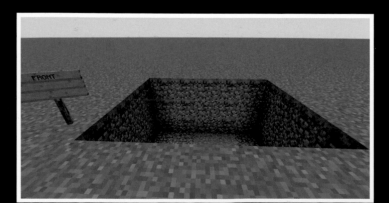

2. At the bottom of the hole, 1 block in from the left side, place a chest. This is where all the customer payments will end up.

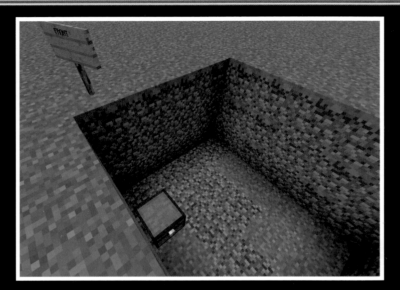

3. Place two hoppers above the chest. Both hoppers should be pointing down.

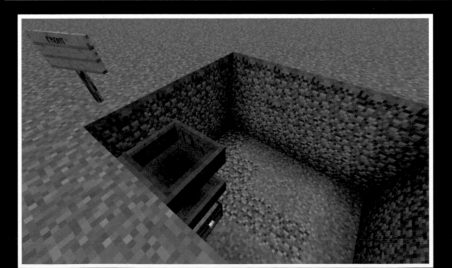

4. Now dig a two-block-long hole in front of the top hopper.

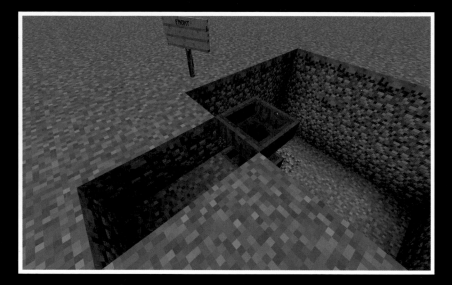

5. Place two hoppers in this trench. Both should point forward to the hopper in front of it. (In this picture, some of the ground is removed so you can see the correct hopper direction.)

6. Place a chest on top of the front-most hopper. This will be where customers put their payment. Ultimately, the payment will be transferred by the hoppers to the bottom chest.

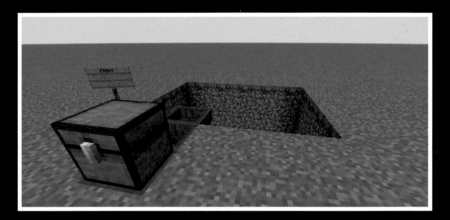

7. The bottom hopper nearest the bottom chest is where you will place items that decide what kind of payment is needed. However, to work in this contraption, this hopper must be disabled from passing items on. To do this, first place a block (I've used lime green wool) next to the bottom chest, and place 1 redstone dust on top of it. This redstone dust, when it is lit up, will power the hopper, stopping it from passing items along.

8. Place a repeater on the ground, pointing toward the green wool. This repeater will help make sure that the signal going to the bottom hopper doesn't get crossed with other redstone signals in the contraption.

9. One block from the repeater, at the back of the 4x5 hole, place another block (I've used blue wool). On the side of the block that faces the repeater, place a redstone torch. The redstone torch powers the block of space that it is in, so its signal can continue through the repeater and to the redstone dust on the green wool, and to the bottom hopper. Also, because the torch is placed on the side of the wool, it can later be powered off by the signal powering the blue wool.

10. Now we are going to place redstone that will allow the bottom hopper to be powered off very briefly, when payment is made, allowing the payment to drop to the bottom chest. First place 2 blocks (I've used pink wool) behind the chest.

11. On the pink wool nearest the chest, place a comparator pointing away from the chest. This comparator will get a signal from the bottom hopper. The strength of the signal depends on the number of items in the hopper. It reaches full strength when the hopper is full.

12. On the second piece of wool, place a repeater pointing away from the comparator. This repeater helps prevent the signal from the comparator from getting mixed up with other signals in the contraption.

13. Place 2 blocks to the right of the comparator (I've used orange wool). On the top of the block closest to the comparator add 1 redstone dust. On the other, place a redstone torch. This torch is sending a full-strength signal to the comparator. Only when the bottom hopper is full will the hopper's signal to the comparator be equal to the side-signal from the torch. And only then will the comparator produce a signal out its front that will run through the repeater.

14. Now we are going to connect the signal that will come from the comparator to the signal that will turn off the hopper. Behind the block holding the repeater on pink wool, place one redstone dust. If a signal comes from the comparator, this redstone will light up, powering off the redstone torch on the blue wool. The signal to the bottom hopper will be stopped for as long as the comparator is sending out a signal.

15. Now we are going to connect the same signal from the comparator to a circuit that will allow items to be delivered to the customer. Right above the dust you just placed, place another block. I've used cyan wool.

16. On the side of the cyan wool that is above the blue wool, place 1 redstone torch.

17. Above the torch you just placed, place another block (I've used pink wool). On top of this, place another redstone torch. This torch will turn off, because it is receiving a signal from the torch below. When the torch below turns off, it will turn on.

18. Place another block above the redstone torch you placed in step 17. (I've used yellow wool here.)

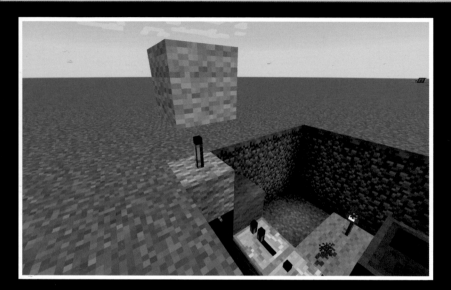

19. Now lay a 3x2 layer of blocks (I've used white wool) as shown.

20. On top of the white wool, place 2 blocks (I've used light blue wool) as shown. These white and light blue wool blocks are used to hold a redstone timer that will deliver goods to the customer.

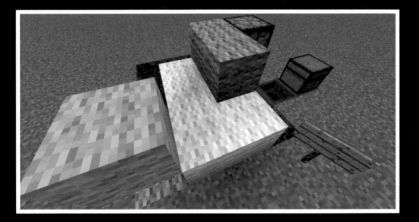

21. Place a comparator pointing toward the front and away from the yellow wool. Right-click it once to set it to "subtract" mode. The front mini-torch on the comparator will light up to show it is in this mode.

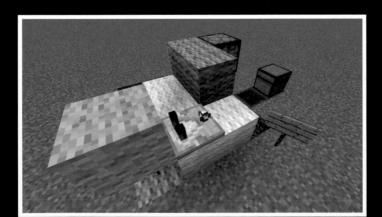

22. Place a repeater pointing toward the side of the comparator.

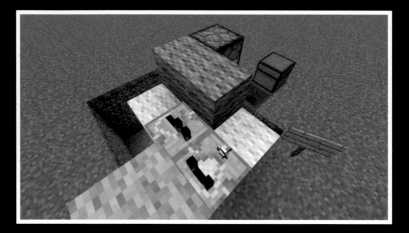

23. Place 4 redstone dust on top of the rest of the white and light blue wool blocks. This creates a circular signal from the comparator, over the light blue wool, to the dropper, to the repeater, and back to the comparator.

24. Almost done! Fill up the dropper with the items you are selling. You can right-click the dropper and drag items from your inventory. (I've used stacks of roasted chicken.)

25. Now, right-click the bottom dropper, above the bottom chest, to open up its inventory. In the leftmost slot, place 63 items of the same type you want for payment. I've used iron ingots, but you could use any stackable item, like emeralds or diamonds. In the four right slots, place 4 wooden swords. Because swords don't stack, they fill up these four slots fully so that they can't be used in the hopper payment transfer. Now the hopper is almost completely full.

26. Your vending machine redstone is done! Try it out by placing payment in the top chest. The same number of for-sale items should pop out of the dropper. If you have any problems, go back and check each step carefully. Look out for the way repeaters and comparators point, and how redstone torches are placed (on a block's top, or on the side of a block).

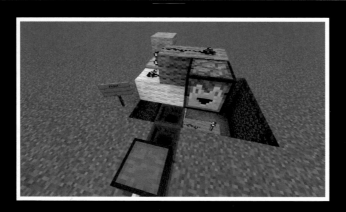

27. Now you can decorate your vending machine. In front of the dropper, place a block of your choice. Decorate it with an item frame and a chicken. The items from the dropper will still pop through to the front of this.

28. Place a wall behind the chest and beside the dropper's decoration to hide the redstone. Add signs to explain what customers should do.

29. Keep decorating until you are satisfied. I've made a store around the vending machine. I used orange and white wool, light-gray stained glass panes, spruce wood blocks, and an acacia wood door. (Plus lots of item frames with roast chicken in them!) In the back, I've enclosed all the redstone in a maintenance area with spruce wood. Inside, there are stairs so you can easily get to the dropper to add goods and to the chest to collect your payment!

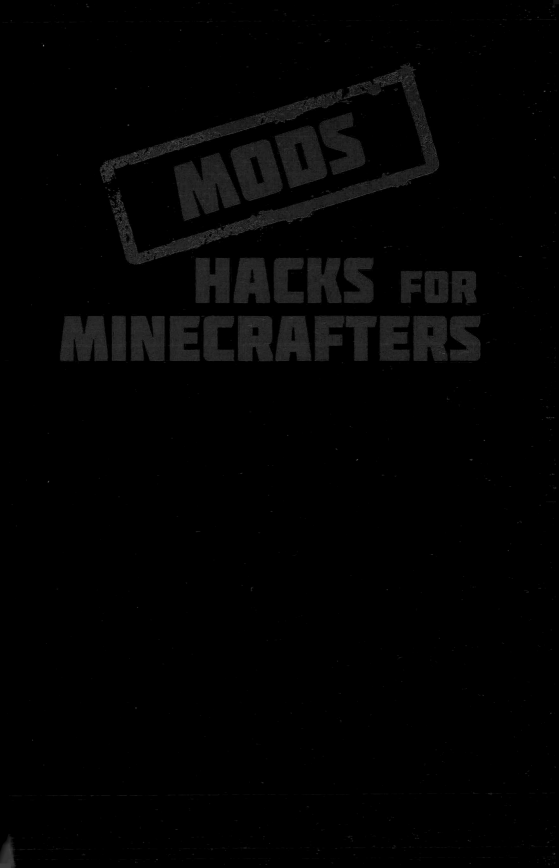

MODS

HACKS FOR
MINECRAFTERS

CHAPTER 1

ALL ABOUT MODS

Welcome to the mad, magical, and high-tech world of modded Minecraft. Modded Minecraft isn't a single game, it's Minecraft modified with the mods you want to play with. You can play with one or a couple of mods, a dozen mods, or a modpack that comes ready with a preset selection of mods.

What Are Mods?

"Mod" is short for "modification," and mods are game programming objects that change the way a game behaves. In Minecraft, mods can change how you farm, how you fight, how you mine, and how (and what) you craft, and more. Some mods are simple and change just one small part of the game. For example, JourneyMap adds a very handy mapping system to Minecraft. Other mods change major aspects of Minecraft. The magical mod Thaumcraft creates a unique type of sorcery, with spells, wands, magic energy, and magical mobs for you to play with. Some more examples are:

- **Simply Jetpacks** lets you craft powered jetpacks to fly around in your world. (This is probably my favorite mod—there's nothing better than flying!)

- **The Twilight Forest** creates an entirely new dimension you can visit by traveling through a special portal. The Twilight Forest dimension has new animals, mobs, boss mobs, dungeons, and more to explore.

- **The Extra Utilities** adds a bunch of interesting and useful items, tools, and blocks, like conveyer belts, to help move captured mobs or items around, and a bunch of power generators for early game power.

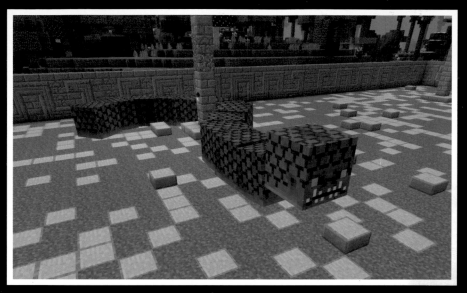

The Twilight Forest mod adds an entirely new dimension to explore, with new boss mobs, biomes, and more.

Mods are made for the PC version of Minecraft, and there are several places you can find them:

- Planet Minecraft (PMC) at planetminecraft.com/resources/mods/

- The Minecraft Forum at minecraftforum.net/forums/mapping-and-modding/minecraft-mods

- Curse at curse.com/mc-mods/minecraft

- Mod authors' websites

Modpacks are collections of mods that are carefully selected to work together, both in balanced gameplay and in technical compatibility. Modpacks are the easiest way to get started playing with mods, because they are easy to download and install. Some modpacks come with a questing system that gives you challenges to accomplish and sometimes rewards when you complete them. Some modpacks have an overall theme or storyline. In the Crash Landing modpack, you are stranded on an unknown planet with a dying spaceship and must battle a very harsh desert environment.

In the classic Crash Landing modpack, you are stranded on a dusty planet and must struggle to survive against a harsh, dry landscape.

You can find and install modpacks using modpack launchers. The most popular modpack launchers are:

- Feed the Beast (FTB) launcher. The Feed the Beast team has produced and gathered a large set of modpacks, along with a launcher, which you can find at their site feed-the-beast.com.

- Curse launcher. The gaming network site has also created a launcher, Curse for Minecrafters, that incorporates Feed the Beast modpacks and others, which you can find at beta.cursevoice.com/games/minecraft. (This launcher is also used for Curse's voice chat application.)

- AT Launcher, available at atlauncher.com.

- Technic Launcher, available at technicpack.net.

Modpack launchers, like the Curse launcher, make installing modpacks easy.

This book will look at some of the most popular mods and mod-packs available and show you how to download them. I'll also show how to get started playing with modpacks. Many of these mods offer so much gameplay, however, that it is likely you'll want even more information on them. In general, you can visit several websites to get more information on how to play. Visit the Curse Minecraft mods site (curse.com/mc-mods/minecraft), the Minecraft Forum (minecraftforum.net). The FTB wiki (ftbwiki.org) and forums (feed-the-beast.com/forum/) also are a great source of information about many mods. Many mods have deeper explanations at their own wiki sites. You can also visit my website at meganfmiller.com for links to these sites and helpful YouTube videos that look at how to play with these mods.

Warning: Mods can change the original Minecraft programming code and you have to be very careful backing up your worlds and installing them. Mods are unsupported by Mojang, the game developers. Even though Mojang has made Minecraft so that it can be modded, if you run into a problem, Mojang can't help you. You'll have to rely on the community of modders and players to help you through technical and gameplay problems.

BEFORE YOU START INSTALLING AND PLAYING WITH MODS, THERE ARE SOME CONCEPTS YOU SHOULD BE FAMILIAR WITH:

Minecraft Versions

Mods are always a little behind vanilla Minecraft. (Vanilla Minecraft is the term that people use to describe playing Minecraft without any mods.) That's because the mod developers must wait till a new stable release of Minecraft is released before they can even begin adapting their existing mods or creating new mods for it. Currently, several mods are available for Minecraft 1.8, but the bulk of mods and modpacks are running on Minecraft 1.7.10.

If you install mods or modpacks individually, you will need to be aware of what version of Minecraft they work with. If you are manually installing mods, you will need to download the right version of Minecraft as well. If you choose to use a custom launcher or modpack launcher, this will be taken care of for you fairly seamlessly. A custom or modpack launcher replaces the Minecraft launcher. (When you run Minecraft, the first window that appears is the Minecraft launcher, not the game itself.) You can use the Minecraft launcher to make and edit gameplay profiles, and each profile can have different settings for the version of Minecraft you play, the amount of RAM memory it uses, and more.

Mod Makers and Downloads

Mods are created by Minecraft fans who come up with an idea for something they'd like to see in Minecraft, program it into a mod, and release the mod for players to freely download and use in their own game. Unlike programmers at Mojang and other game companies, mod authors don't have a full support team helping them. This means that it isn't unusual for bugs to slip through in the programming, so you have to be careful to make backups of worlds you don't want to lose.

Many mod designers make a little bit of money from advertising that is placed on the download sites they use. If you use a mod author's site to download a mod, you need to keep an eye out for the advertisements. The advertisements often look like they are the real links to the mod but may instead download unwanted software to your PC. If you are taken to an ad.fly website for the download, wait for the timer on the top right to count down and then click the **Skip Ad** button on the top right. Because it can be very difficult to tell the difference between an advertisement and the real download link, I recommend downloading the mod if possible from Curse first, and then donating a small amount to the mod author directly.

When you download individual mods, you are likely to come across web pages that are loaded with advertisements that look like download links. Be careful. With ad-fly sites, like this one, you want to wait several seconds until the **Skip Ad** button appears at the top right, then click that.

Regardless, seriously consider sending some support to mod makers. You can usually find a **Donate** button on their websites or on the Minecraft Forum page. Even a dollar, donated by many players, adds up to help the mod maker, and lets them know their work is appreciated.

You can also help a mod author by signing up to be a beta tester. The Minecraft Forum, at minecraftforum.net, is a central location to discover mods that have been released and are still being worked on. Developers will post announcements here saying that they are looking for beta testers for their mod.

Backups

Mods work by changing some of the programming code in Minecraft. There are thousands of mods, and it isn't unusual for mods to not work well with each other. And there are mods that are buggy and can corrupt your world.

All of this means that if you are manually installing mods (and even if you're not), regularly backup your worlds. To do this, go to your Minecraft game directory and make a backup of the folder named **saves**. In the saves folder are all the files for each world you play. In Windows, this folder is typically located at C:\Users\Megan\AppData\Roaming\minecraft. If you have trouble finding the saves folder, start the Minecraft launcher and click **Edit Profile**. In the Edit Profile window, click the **Open Game Dir** button at the bottom to open your Minecraft directory.

The files for your Minecraft worlds are in your Minecraft game directory's **saves** folder. You can copy the entire folder to another location to back it up.

Modded Multiplayer

This book looks at playing mods in single-player worlds. However, you can find servers that offer modded play. In modded multiplayer, both the server and the client (you) must have mods installed. Most modded multiplayer servers use one of the popular modpacks, such as a Feed the Beast modpack or the Tekkit modpack (available from the Technic launcher).

As I mentioned earlier, mod authors work and distribute their mods for free. They don't have teams of developers and other support to help them, so they can't provide support to users the same way large gaming companies like EA (Electronic Arts) can do. They also can't debug their work against every possible scenario. If you are having technical or gameplay difficulties, there are several places to look for help. In addition to the sites mentioned earlier, look at the mod's page at Planet Minecraft (planetminecraft.com/) and at Curse (curse.com/mc-mods/minecraft). Check to see if you have downloaded the right versions and all required mods, and look for any troubleshooting FAQs or discussions forums at the mod author's website. The community message board site reddit.com also has a large community of Minecraft players who have already discussed the same problems. Of course, you can also try searching Google with your specific problem, such as "Minecraft Twilight Forest portal not working."

CHAPTER 2

INSTALLING MODS

There are three main ways to install mods:

1. Individually, using the Forge mod (not recommended except for advanced computer users).

2. Individually, using a custom launcher.

3. As packs of mods, using a modpack launcher (recommended).

First, a key concept in installing mods is making sure you use a separate instance of Minecraft for mods. An instance of Minecraft is a full and separate installation of Minecraft, including the main Minecraft program file, the minecraft.jar file, and any related files and folders for worlds, resource packs, and more. Using separate instances means that any problems a mod causes will be limited to affecting the single instance it is used in.

Manual/Forge Installation

Forge is a very widely used mod that is used to install and manage mods. It also provides an application programming interface (API) that helps modders create mods. An API is a set of programming tools for working with a specific program. All of this means that mods using Forge tend to work well together. You need to install Forge in order to use any of the Forge-created mods.

However, what Forge doesn't do is automatically create new instances of Minecraft, and this means that your Minecraft application is vulnerable to being corrupted accidentally by a mod, so I won't recommend installing mods individually using Forge unless you have advanced computer skills.

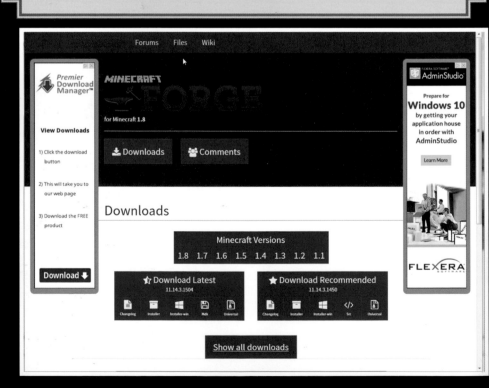

Forge is the mod that allows lots of mods to work well together. If you are downloading Forge manually, you need to make sure you are getting the right version for the version of Minecraft you will use.

Basically, the Forge process is to download and run the Minecraft Forge installer from files.minecraftforge.net and then place zipped mod files that you have downloaded into your mods folder. The mods folder is located in your Minecraft game directory. But, as I've said, if you are new to mods or aren't an advanced computer user, I don't recommend this, as it is very easy to get something wrong both in downloading and in installation.

Installing Mods with a Custom Launcher

You can use a custom launcher like MultiMC to help create and manage mods. You still need to find and download mods individually, but the launcher will help you separate modded worlds from each other and your vanilla worlds. You still need to maintain caution when downloading mods, both to avoid fake advertising downloads and infected files. If you're ready for this, you can follow the instructions for working with the MultiMC launcher in the Appendix.

The MultiMC launcher helps you create different instances of Minecraft, but you still need to download mods individually.

Installing modpacks with a modpack launcher is the easiest way by far to start playing with Minecraft mods and is what I recommend for beginning modded gameplay. All you do, basically, is download and run the modpack launcher. When you start the launcher, you can select which modpack you want to play with, and the launcher will install the mods and create the directories and Minecraft instances you need to keep everything working and separate.

In addition, there are strong communities that maintain the top modpack launchers, and along with forums and documentation, it is easier to find help for technical issues when you are using a modpack launcher.

Four of the most popular modpack launchers are the Curse launcher, the ATLauncher, the Feed the Beast (FTB) launcher, and the Technic launcher. They are all free to use. Each of these modpack launchers have different modpacks you can install, although some modpacks appear in several launchers. The FTB modpacks are being integrated into the Curse launcher, so you will find the FTB modpacks in the Curse launcher. In all of these launchers you will find settings to adjust the RAM memory used and the initial game window size. They will also keep your Minecraft instances separate and allow you to install vanilla Minecraft as well, so that you can use the launcher for all your Minecraft games. You will also need to add your Minecraft game profile to each launcher so that it can verify your account.

----

1. Go to the Curse website (curse.com) and download the Curse for Minecraft installer (at beta.cursevoice.com/games/minecraft).

2. When the download is complete, run the installer.

3. When the launcher is finished installing, run the launcher. You will need to register a new Curse account if you don't already have one.

4. To open the Minecraft areas of the launcher, click the **Minecraft** tab at the top. If you are prompted to install additional items on this tab as shown, do so.

5. In the launcher, you can click **Browse All Modpacks** or **Browse FTB Modpacks** to see what modpacks can be installed. Once you've found a modpack you want to play, click the **Install** button on the modpack's icon.

1. Go to the Feed the Beast website (feed-the-beast.com) and click **Download Now** on the home page. Download the .jar or .exe files for PC or the .jar file for Mac.

2. Run the .exe or .jar file after it is downloaded to run the installer. It will download the base files you need and automatically open the FTB launcher for you.

3. In the launcher, you can click the **FTB modpacks** or the **3rd party modpacks** tab at the top to browse modpacks available. You will need to add your Minecraft game profile using the **Create Profile** button.

4. When you've selected a modpack you'd like to play, click **Launch** to download the files and play the modpack. For very large modpacks, it may take some time to download all the files.

You install other launchers, like the AT launcher and the Technic launcher in pretty much exactly the same way. Download the installer or launcher app and run it. In the launcher, you can select which modpack you want to run. When you start or select the modpack for the first time, the modpack's files will download. You'll find the AT launcher at atlauncher.com and the Technic launcher at technicpack.net.

CHAPTER 3

MUST-HAVE MODS

Everyone playing modded Minecraft has their favorite mods. But there are some mods you feel like you can't play without, once you've experienced their genius. The must-have mods below are favorites of mine and many other Minecrafters. They are some of the most downloaded mods and often included in modpacks.

These must-haves fix common Minecraft annoyances or frustrations, or make things simpler in a modded world. Have you ever forgotten where that desert village is? Or wasted too much time waiting for a large oak's leaf blocks to despawn? Can't remember that recipe for an enchantment table? These mods solve those little irks and more.

Not Enough Items (NEI)

Author: chicken_bones

Not Enough Items (NEI) transforms the inventory interface you get when you press **E** in Minecraft. It gives you an overlay of all the blocks and items available in Minecraft and any installed mods. You can page through or search the list.

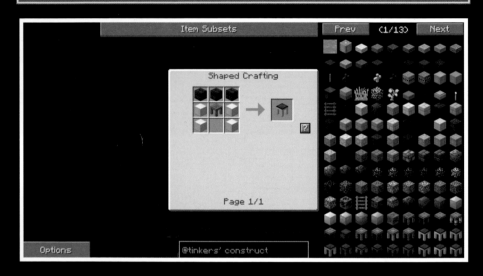

To search for all the items a mod adds, type @ and the mod name in the search box.

The brilliance of NEI is that you can easily find recipes for any item, as well as any recipes an item is used in. If you hover over an item in NEI's interface and press **R**, NEI will show you the crafting recipe for that item. If you make the item in a smelter or other contraption (like getting stone from smelting cobble), NEI will show that as well. And if you press **U**, NEI will show you the recipes that the item is used in.

This is great for vanilla Minecraft, but in modded Minecraft, where you can have thousands of craftable items with different recipes and machines, it's a must.

What's especially awesome is this: if you are working with the crafting table, NEI can automatically fill the grid with ingredients you need. To do this, you have to find the recipe in NEI, select it, and then shift-click the question mark beside the recipe. If you have the crafting ingredients in your personal inventory, NEI will fill the crafting grid with the ingredients so you can just drag your crafted item immediately from the grid. To fill the crafting grid with previews of what's needed, simply click the question mark.

Another fantastic feature of NEI is the mob-spawning indicator. Press **F7** and blocks will be highlighted with a yellow X if a mob can spawn there at night and a red X if a mob can spawn at any time. This lets you know exactly where to put torches or other lights.

NEI has become such a staple that modders have created additional add-on mods, like NEI Integration and NEI Add-ons, that help with crafting recipes from other mods.

In NEI World options, you can play in a cheat mode that allows you to access any item. You can also use buttons for changing the weather, setting the time of day, and the "magnet." The magnet lets any objects you drop accidentally zoom right back to your inventory.

Simply Jetpacks

Author: tonius111

Jetpacks are a great way to avoid the somewhat nastier mobs you'll often find in modded Minecraft.

When I start a modded world, one of my first goals, after setting up a base, food resources, and a mining operation, is to obtain a jetpack. Having a jetpack, for me, means I feel much safer. I can fly away from any monster that surprises me, take a moment to breathe, and then kill it or figure out my escape. This is a massive boon in the Nether, which, in a modpack, might be much more dangerous than the vanilla Nether. A jetpack also makes it easier to build neater structures. And, of course, jetpacks are just awesome by themselves.

Simply Jetpacks is actually an add-on mod for another popular tech mod, Thermal Expansion, which itself works with the mods Thermal Foundation and CoHCore (a code library), so you'll have to have those three mods installed together. These mods add ores and ore-processing machines to Minecraft. They're pretty essential, too, and we'll look at them in the Tech Mods chapter.

To craft a jetpack, you do need some resources and special machines to replenish its energy so it doesn't feel that cheaty. The lowest level jetpack is within your reach after a trip to the Nether and gathering some resources (a variety of fairly common materials: ores, glass, sulfur, redstone, etc.).

To run the jetpacks added by Simply Jetpacks, you'll need the energetic infuser machine from Thermal Expansion to replenish its energy. You'll also need a power source for the infuser, like this survivalist generator from Extra Utilities.

No more waiting for the leaves of your chopped tree to despawn. Chop the tree and the leaves crumble within seconds. This is a small mod that does one thing perfectly. Beware, though, once you have gotten used to fast leaf decay, it's very hard to go back to vanilla.

Chop down a tree and its leaves disappear almost immediately with the Fast Leaf Decay mod.

Inventory Tweaks

Author: Kobata

With Inventory Tweaks, when you open a chest, you can click the buttons at the top to sort the contents. Press the ellipses button to open up Inventory Tweaks options.

Like Waila and NEI, Inventory Tweaks adds some incredibly useful functions to inventories. Automatic refill means that when you are using blocks, like placing cobble to make a wall, and your stack runs out of that block, your inventory slot will automatically refill with more of the block if it is somewhere in your inventory. Repair-friendly refill means that if your pick breaks, its inventory slot will refill with the same type of pick if you have one in inventory.

In Inventory Tweaks options, you can turn on and off auto-refill and repair-friendly refill.

Waila (What Am I Looking At) is a small mod that gives you information about blocks. It will tell you the name of the block you are looking at and what mod it is from. This may seem fairly useless in vanilla Minecraft, but in a modpack with hundreds of mods, each with new blocks and items, it's extremely helpful.

Waila shows you the name of the object you're looking at and the mod it is from.

If you also install the add-on mod Waila Harvestability, it will tell you the best tool to use to break the block in front of you. This is a huge help when you are working with the more complex tiers of tools of Tinkers' Construct.

With Waila Harvestability mod, you'll also see what tool you can use to harvest the block.

Tinkers' Construct (also referred to as Tinkers or tcon) overhauls the tool and weapon system of Minecraft. It has become such a staple in modded Minecraft that you will find it in many modpacks.

With tcon, you have many more choices than wood, iron, gold, or diamond to make your tools and weapons from. Tinkers adds new ores to the Overworld, like aluminum, copper, and tin, as well as a few new ores to the Nether, like ardite and cobalt. It also adds some gravel forms of ores.

This Tinkers' pick is made from a manyullyn pickaxe head (purple), a paper rod, and a pink slime binding. Extra effects are added with a ball of moss for autorepair (green), speed with redstone, and luck (fortune) with lapis.

With Tinkers' Construct, you can find gravel versions of ores in the open as well as underground. To work with the ores, and cast them into weapon parts, you first make a smeltery. A smeltery will melt the ores you put inside and also allows you to create special alloys from combinations of ores. Once melted, you pour out your metals in basins, to get blocks of a metal, or into casts, to make weapon and tool parts or ingots.

To melt ores, you'll have to make a smeltery. You can find the beginnings of a smeltery in villages.

Tinkers' tools don't disappear when their durability is used up. Instead, they "break" and stop working. You can then repair them using one or more ingots or units of their base material, like iron or gold.

There's a huge variety of Tinkers' weapons and tools. In addition to regular Minecraft tools, you can make different types of swords, daggers, broadaxes, lumber axes, scythes, crossbows, and more. Out of these, my current favorites are the hammer, which you use like a pick and mines a 3x3 hole, and the excavator, which mines sand, gravel, and dirt, also in 3x3 blocks. These two tools make manual mining a very sweet and speedy activity.

Tinkers' Construct also adds some slime to your world: small slime sky islands made of slime dirt and slime grass, and purple and green congealed slime, with slime trees and blue slime mobs. Occasionally a King Slime boss mob will spawn and jump over the island edge to fall into your neighborhood. The King Slime has 100 health points and will sometimes drop the rare King Slime Hammer, a decent weapon that can deal 7 hearts of damage.

A slime sky island added with the Tinkers' mod.

JourneyMap

Author: TechMap

> JourneyMap adds a small map to your Minecraft game window and a large map screen you can access by pressing **J**. The maps show not only where you are, but also any mobs that are nearby. Underground, it will show features like lava and water. You can configure JourneyMap heavily, from the map size and zoom level, to what mobs it shows.

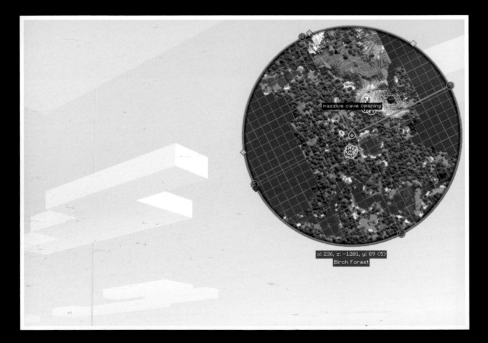

JourneyMap adds a small map to the top left. It also lets you add waypoints, which appear on your screen as beams of light.

Best of all, you can add waypoints, a type of in-game bookmark, to your world. A waypoint places a colored beam of light in the world at your choice of location, and you can name the waypoints to remember what they mark. To quickly set a waypoint, press **B**. You can see waypoints from far away, and labels show the waypoint name and how far away they are. This is perfect for marking your portal in the Nether.

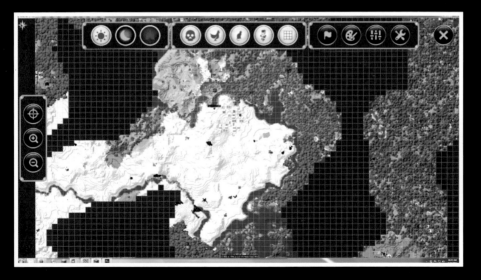

Press **J** to see JourneyMap's full-screen map, where you can also adjust settings and access the list of waypoints you have created.

Extra Utilities

Author: RWTema

The Extra Utilities mod is a collection of assorted items and blocks that can be extremely useful, from early game power generators and pipes that are easy to craft, to conveyer belts and spikes you can use to create mob traps. Some of the top, for me, are:

- Golden Bag of Holding. This bag lets you carry a double-chest's worth of more stuff in your personal inventory.

- Builder's Wand. The Builder's Wand lets you place 8 blocks at a time, of whatever block it is pointing at, in the next layer in the wand's direction. You do need to have enough matching blocks in your inventory. The Super Builder's Wand can place up to 49 blocks.

- Angel Block. The Angel Block can be placed anywhere in the world, for example, in mid-air, so you can easily start a construction in the sky without having to build a column up first.

The conveyer belts from Extra Utilities make it very easy to force mobs into your mob grinder

Optifine

Author: sp614x

If there's one mod that vanilla players use, it's Optifine. It's a utility mod that improves the Minecraft fps, or framerate (how fast the game runs), as well as visuals. It improves lighting and how textures connect, and gives many more options under the Minecraft Visual Settings screen. There are three versions—Lite, Standard, and Ultra. The version that is designed to work best with other mods is Standard.

CHAPTER 4

MODS FOR ADVENTURE AND RPG

Mods for adventure and RPG (role-playing games) add new biomes and dimensions to explore. Some of these mods change the way villages and villagers behave, and others bring fantastic new flora and fauna to your Minecraft world. These are a few of the most popular; they all work with Forge, and you'll find many in popular modpacks like FTB Infinity.

Biomes O' Plenty

Author: Glitchfiend

You can explore over 70 new biomes with the Biomes O' Plenty mod—from Alps and Badlands to Tropical Rainforest and Wetlands. In addition to giving us new flowers, shrubs, even new dirt varieties, the mod adds over 20 types of trees that grow in the biomes, like Bamboo trees and giant Redwood trees. These new trees are also great for builders, as their logs give lots of new color options for wood planks, stairs, and slabs.

Watch out for the quicksand added by Biomes O' Plenty (although it can work out in your favor, as it can trap mobs as well). It's slightly darker than regular sand, and it can suffocate you. To get out of quicksand, move to the edge and break the quicksand blocks beneath you.

A few biomes are magical, such as the Mystic Grove biome, with magic trees and glowflowers. The Biomes O' Plenty mod also includes five new biomes in the Nether, including the Boneyard (the first image in this chapter). In the Boneyard, you can find gravestones and giant bones sticking out of the netherrack.

Biome's O Plenty biomes include Sacred Springs (A), Canyon (B), Bamboo Forest (C), and Jade Cliffs (D).

Tip: To use this mod, you need to create a new Minecraft world with its World Type set to Biomes O' Plenty.

Mo' Creatures

Author: DrZhark

This mod adds over 40 animal and hostile monster mobs to your game, including birds, insects, ocean life, big golems, wraiths, werewolves, and the dragonlike wyverns. You'll have to build your own zoo though! Some of the mobs can be tamed and kept as pets and others—like the elephants—you can also ride.

Mo' Creatures adds passive and hostile mobs to the game, including big cats, foxes, elephants, and raccoons.

JurassiCraft

Authors: kashmoney360, JTGhowk137, LieutenantGhost, TheDurpiDoedric

Get your prehistoric on with this mod inspired by the Jurassic Park movies. First, you'll have to mine to find the fossils and amber for dino DNA. Then you'll need to craft some specialized machines: a DNA extractor to get that ancient DNA and a cultivator to create the precious dino eggs.

These are the dinosaur fossil blocks you have to mine in order to create dinosaurs.

There are over 30 prehistoric creatures here, from the giant brachiosaurs, triceratops, raptors, and T. rex, to dodos and coelacanths. If you are dino mad, you might also want to try out another prehistoric creatures mod, Archaeology and Fossils Revival.

Twilight Forest

Author: Benimatic

If you like to explore new lands, fight powerful and strange mobs, and find hidden loot and treasure, Twilight Forest may be the mod for you. This very popular mod adds an entirely new enchanted and eerie dimension, similar to the Nether or the End. The Twilight Forest is cram-packed with adventurous content: new biomes, dungeons, mazes, castles, animals, boss mobs, trees, insects, and more.

The Twilight Forest adds an entirely new dimension that is permanently dusk.

The mobs, structures, and plants in Twilight Forest are all beautifully created and just exploring the land is an awesome experience. To get there, all you need to do is make a 2x2 hole, fill it with water, surround it with flowers, and throw in a diamond. After a few moments and a bang, the water pool will turn into your portal to the Twilight Forest. If you are going alone, make sure you have enchanted armor, weapons, and potions because some of the mobs in the Twilight Forest are quite powerful.

Mystcraft

Author: XCompWiz

The Mystcraft mod is inspired by the Myst series of video games and books. In Mystcraft, you write, or craft, enchanted books to create and travel to new worlds called Ages. You can create random Ages by creating a book with a blank page, or you can customize a new Age by including pages that describe a feature of the world. World features range from the type and organization of biomes to the color of skies, types of ores, and more.

In Mystcraft, you create new worlds by crafting a mystical book using your writing desk.

Random Ages have a high chance of being unstable or dangerous. An unstable world has negative effects, like poisoning, spontaneous explosions, or decay, which makes the Age self-destruct.

Clicking a descriptive book transports you to a platform in the new world.

You start by creating a descriptive book to create an Age. To travel to that Age, right-click that book to open it and click on the black square. Be careful, because without a linking book back to the Overworld or a sky fissure, a natural portal, you can get permanently stuck in your world.

To find pages with world features, locate the libraries in your new world. Inside are lecterns with new pages, and a hidden chest.

Minecraft Comes Alive

Author: WildBamaBoy

Minecraft Comes Alive (MCA) brings new life to your villages. Gone are the dour and bald villagers; in are new male and female villagers wearing player-like skins and assigned different personalities. They'll greet you in chat and you can right-click them to bring up a whole new set of interactions, including chat, joke, gift, trade, hire, and more.

Depending on your choosing an appropriate interaction with a villager (hint: don't joke too much with a serious character), you'll gain relationship points (hearts) with the villager, up to five red hearts that can improve to five gold hearts. After you've earned enough hearts, you can give a villager a crafted engagement ring, and then a crafted wedding ring. Once you're married, you can "procreate" for a baby item. After ten minutes, right-click the baby item and you'll have a child. What's great about the children is that you can assign them chores, like farming or fishing. They may whine, but if they have the right tools and items, they'll do it!

When you first start a world with MCA, you'll be given a crystal ball in your inventory. To begin your adventure, right-click the crystal ball to enter a library room, and you'll be given a choice of how to start with MCA. Start with a ready-made family (spouse and 0–2 kids), living in a village, living alone, or none of the above. You can also bypass the crystal ball, or choose none of the above and wait until you're ready to find a village and start interacting.

CHAPTER 5

MODS O' MAGIC

Minecraft's magical mods show how creative the Minecraft community is. Each of the four main magical mods—Thaumcraft, Botania, Witchery, and Blood Magic—bring a different system of magic to your world, with their own unique contraptions and ways to enhance your world with special effects and powers. These are all beautifully designed mods with excellent animations, objects, items, and gameplay.

Thaumcraft

Author: azanor

Thaumcraft is the ultimate magical Minecraft magical mod. It opens up hours of new gameplay as you learn the art of sorcery. You begin by making a simple wand, your guidebook (the Thaumonomicon), and a special device—the Thaumometer. With the Thaumometer, you can see and research the magical energy (essentia) present in all items and blocks, as well as find the magical energy nodes in the world around you.

Thaumcraft's Goggles of Revealing will show you where magical energy nodes are in the Minecraft world.

In Thaumcraft, you use the Thaumometer to research what magical aspects make up each item and object.

You have to research the right Minecraft blocks and items in order to progress in the Thaumcraft world, and there is a mini-game in a research table to help you learn more. As you gain more knowledge, more and more of Thaumcraft's magical recipes, abilities, and crafting will open up to you. You will be able to infuse objects with magical abilities at your Infusion Altar, distill potent energies from common blocks, and much more.

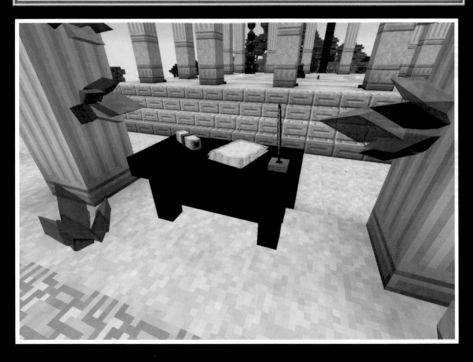

You can research new knowledge (of magical blocks, procedures, contraptions) by playing a mini-game using the research table.

Thaumcraft adds new trees, plants, ores, wands, cauldrons, staves, and contraptions. Especially fun are the golems—little utility mobs you can program to perform simple tasks for you, like planting trees or keeping your cauldron full of bubbling water.

The popular mod Witchery opens up a more plant-based type of magic. Instead of working with natural energies, the way Thaumcraft does, Witchery uses the magical power of the plants around you. You can make small dolls called poppets to protect you and write glyphs in a circle to perform magical rites. You'll have a witch's oven, cauldron, spinning wheel, altar, and brewing kettle to craft your potent charms. You can even bind a cat, owl, or toad to you to become your familiar, making you even more powerful.

The Witchery altar gains power from the trees and plants around it.

Witchery is a complex and deep mod, creating a world of play with covens, werewolves, vampires, curses, spirits, and more. It adds larger villages to your world that are often walled. In these larger villages you can find several books to guide you in Witchery skills at bookshops, as well as witchcraft ingredients at the apothecary.

Witchery adds many mobs, one of which is the winged monkey which you can tame and have fight alongside you.

Larger, walled villages are also added by Witchery.

Blood Magic sounds gruesome, and it kind of is. It's also a fantastic mod, if you don't take the "blood" idea too seriously. Think of it as "life essence." With this mod, you take the health points of yourself and mobs, store it as a type of energy in an altar and orbs, and use it to create magical instruments, effects, and rituals.

There are several tiers of Blood Altar, which increase in size and power—this is Tier 5.

You start by crafting a Blood Altar, Sacrificial Orb, and a Weak Blood Orb. You'll use these materials to make upgrades to your altars and orbs, gather more life essence for your altar and Soul Network, and create magical tokens like sigils for creating infinite water, flying, fast mining and farming, and more. As you perfect your tactic for gathering and storing life essence, you'll be able to perform more powerful (and expensive) rites and rituals. The Ritual of Magnetism pulls up ores in the ground (in a certain range) without you having to do any digging!

The Sigil of the Phantom Bridge creates a temporary black bridge beneath you as you walk.

The magic you use with Botania is probably the most cheerful of the magical mods. It's based on magical flower petals. But don't be fooled—the Botania magic is also powerful, and it is a complex and engaging mod. In Botania, you work with an energy called Mana, which you get from special mystical flowers.

The Botania mod adds a variety of highly detailed and colorful flowers to use in your magic.

You gather the Mana from your flowers in a Mana Pool, which you then use to craft new items. Or you can distribute the Mana with special mechanisms to your Runic Altar, where you can create even more unique items.

Magic flowers generate Mana, which can be sent to collect in a Mana Pool.

Start by creating the guide book, the Lexica Botania, by crafting a book with a sapling together. This will give you a tutorial and information on everything you can do with Botania magic. Also, shift right-click on a Botania object with the Lexica to get more information about that object.

You can use the Runic Altar to craft new magical items using Mana as a source of power.

Morph doesn't bring a system of magic to Minecraft, but it does give you one awesome magical ability. With Morph, whenever you kill a mob, you gain the power to transform into that creature. You'll look like that creature and move like it too. Kill a bat and you'll be able to fly, kill a spider and you can float up walls. Use the left and right bracket keys to open up the menu to choose which creature you want to look like!

The Morph mod gives you the ability to morph into any creature you have killed. Select one from your list and you'll change into their size and be able to move like that creature.

CHAPTER 6

THE TECH MODS

Minecraft tech is all about crafting: bigger, better, and faster. There are machines to automate tasks like farming, chopping trees, and even breeding animals. There are pipes so you can transfer items, liquids, and energy. And there are storage systems that can hold so much more than a double chest. So forget mining with your enchanted diamond pickaxe. How would you like a quarry to dig out a 25x25 hole to bedrock, remove all the ores, and then smelt and sort them for you?

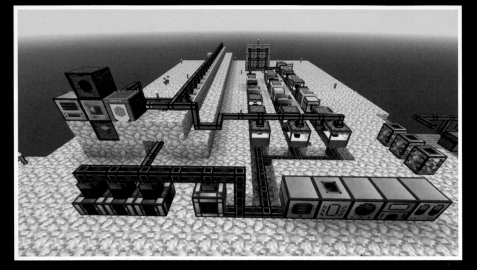

A basic ore-processing and energy set-up in a skyblock: cobble is turned into lava, which Dynamos convert into energy that is sent to power ore-crushers and sifters, which is smelted into ingots and packaged into blocks.

Like all the top mods in Minecraft, these tech mods have been well-thought-out and balanced by their creators. Balanced means that you won't be an auto-diamond machine made from two logs that outputs hundreds of diamonds for you. You have to gather resources and do some complicated crafting in order to get the contraptions that are the most advanced and profitable.

Another key concept in the tech mods is energy. In vanilla Minecraft, the only energy you need is the wood, coal, lava, or blaze rods you put into your furnace to smelt metals and cook food. High tech machines in these mods need much more power—power from generators, steam turbines, windmills, solar panels, and even nuclear reactors. (And you'll have to build them!)

There are three main types of Minecraft power:

- **Minecraft Joules (MJ)**: Used primarily by BuildCraft.

- **Redstone Flux (RF)**: Used by most mods.

- **Energy Units (EU)**: Used by IndustrialCraft 2 and its add-ons.

As a beginner, what you need to know about energy is that occasionally a machine from one mod will have difficulty being powered with a generator from another mod. Thermal Expansion's energy conduits will transfer between MJ and RF, and there are some mods that provide power converters. The easiest way to avoid needing power conversion is to use power generators and contraptions from the same mod.

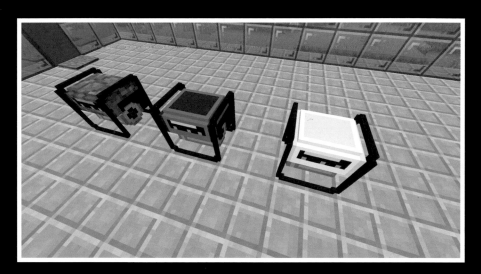

The Extra Utilities mod provides generators good for early game power, including the Survivalist Generator (vanilla fuel), the Ender Generator (Ender pearls), and the Culinary Generator (various foods, including zombie brains).

These technical mods can have some very complicated mechanics behind them, and you can find endless discussions online at forums like reddit.com and the Minecraft forum about the ins and outs of their capabilities, efficiencies, conversions, and more. However, you can get started easily with all of these mods and pretty much do whatever you need to without getting bogged down in the details. And if you are into details, there are lots available for you!

BuildCraft

Authors: Covertlaguar, buildcraftchildsplay

BuildCraft is a long-standing, widely used, engineering focused mod. It provides a number of machines for gathering and managing large quantities of resources, such as a quarry for mining, a pump to get and transfer liquids (like oil), a refinery to process your oil, and more. There are a variety of pipes to use for different tasks, and robots for planting, harvesting, shoveling, chopping trees, and more. Pipes in BuildCraft are see-through, so you can see your little blocks of cobble, dirt, ores, and more travelling to their destinations.

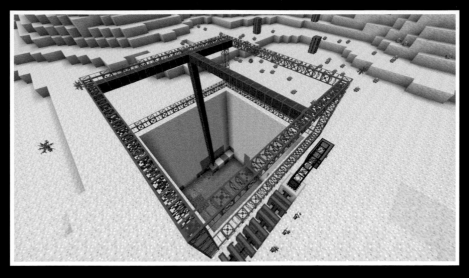

A BuildCraft quarry will dig straight down to bedrock for you and pump out the blocks it mines.

The BuildCraft MJ power comes from engines: from low-power Redstone Engines to the most powerful Combustion Engines that need a liquid fuel. Beware: the Combustion Engines can also explode, if you aren't careful in handling them properly.

Thermal Expansion Series

Authors: TeamCoFH, KingLemming, jadedcat, ZeldoKavira

Designed initially to work as machines to complement BuildCraft, Thermal Expansion has grown to be a robust must-have tech mod in itself. You'll want to grab all three mods in the series: Thermal Expansion (machines, power, storage), Thermal Dynamics (transport pipes), and Thermal Foundation (a requirement for the others, this provides resources like ores).

Thermal Expansion machines are very popular for their ore and material processing.

While BuildCraft helps gather resources like oil and rocks, Thermal Expansion machines primarily help process ores and materials. A Redstone Furnace can smelt faster than a vanilla furnace, and an Induction Smelter can combine ores and materials into alloys. A Pulverizer will crush ores (and more), a Magma Crucible melts stuff, and a Fluid Transposer will take fluids and insert them into special containers. The machines are all upgradeable: a base crafting component—a machine frame—comes in four levels. The base level allows you to start making these machines while you still don't have a ton of resources. As you gather more and more exotic items and resources (from the Nether and elsewhere), you can upgrade to more powerful machines. There are a variety of power generators called Dynamos, energy cells that act like power backups, plus pipes for transporting liquids, items, and energy. It's all terribly good fun, as you learn to hook all these up together, amass crates and chests of resources, and craft your jetpack to fly around the Nether.

Minefactory Reloaded

Authors: Skyboy026, TeamCoFH

Minefactory Reloaded (MFR) adds more machines to help automate a lot of Minecraft tasks, such as fishing, planting, fertilizing, harvesting, milking, shearing, animal slaughter, and even enchanting. In general, the machines work on a single block in front of them, and you craft upgrades to insert into the machine so that they cover a wider area.

You can use two machines to make a very easy mob farm and grinder. First, you can catch a mob with a safari net, place the safari net in an auto-spawner. With power, the auto-spawner will spawn out the same type of mobs, then the mob grinder will kill the spawned mobs and collect their drops.

MFR also adds rubber trees and the processing of rubber into plastic and plastic sheets for crafting its machines. Other materials MFR adds are liquid meat, pink slime, sludge, and sewage.

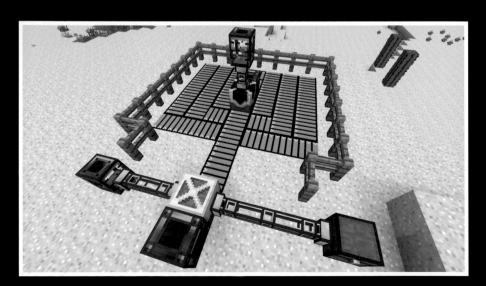

An MFR auto-spawner and grinder can make setting up mob farms easy.

Applied Energistics 2

Authors: AlgorithmX2, Cisien, thatsIch, fireball1725, akarso

Applied Energistics 2 (AE2) is an amazing mod that takes the concept of translating matter to energy and back again, and transforms crafting and storage. With AE2, you can transfer your material resources, from apples to zombie flesh, into "energy equivalents" and store them on computer-like hard drives called ME (Material Energy) drives. Building an ME network allows you to input and output resources at a distance, and a crafting monitor lets you craft and access resources from your drives on the network. Add a crafting CPU (Central Processing Unit), a few other gadgets, lots of power, and you can direct your crafting terminal to autocraft 100 pistons for you in about a minute. Nice. The mod's visuals are also beautifully designed and animated.

An AE2 setup for an ME network includes an ME controller, an ME drive with disks, crafting CPUs, a molecular assembler, and various monitors.

JABBA
- - - - - - -
Authors: ProfMobius, taelnia

If there's one thing the tech mods give you, it's tons and tons of resources—wood from automated tree farms, bones and mob drops from mob grinders, and blocks of metals from mining and smelting operations. Until you get your ME system up and running, you're going to need ways to store this stuff, and a hundred wooden chests is a lot to deal with. Here's where JABBA (Just Another Better Barrel Attempt) comes in. JABBA lets you fairly cheaply create barrels that will hold 64 stacks of a single item. You can upgrade the barrels to hold tons more by adding Structural Upgrades to upgrade slots, and then Storage Upgrades in the new slots. You can use a JABBA Dolly to move barrels (and regular chests) around without dropping their contents. And you can also add special upgrades, like redstone and hopper functionality.

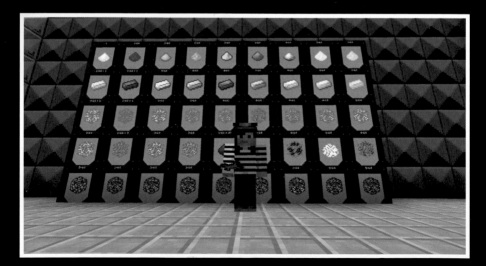

JABBA barrels can hold at minimum 64 stacks of a single item and be upgraded from there.

Other Tech Mods of Note:

These aren't the only great tech mods. Other mods you should seriously consider playing around with are:

- **IndustrialCraft2 (IC2):** Automation and factories.

- **Forestry:** Farming tech, with an emphasis on trees and bees you can cultivate into unique species.

- **Railcraft:** An in-depth overhaul of rails and carts.

- **ComputerCraft:** Adds computers and programmable robots called turtles.

- **EnderIO:** Ore processing, resource transportation, power.

- **ProjectRed:** Adds new functionality and gadgets for you to create your original contraptions. Big Reactors: If you just can't get enough power, go nuclear.

One of the smaller reactors from the mod Big Reactors. It uses yellorium as fuel, is cooled by gelid cryotheum, and outputs power and cyanite as waste.

CHAPTER 7

MODS FOR BUILDERS

There's a bounty of mods that can help Minecraft architects, interior designers, and mapmakers perfect their creations. Some add to the blocks you can use to decorate and build with; others make the act of building large structures much, much easier.

Chisel 2

Authors: TheCricket26, Drullkus

Chisel 2 adds many new textures to existing blocks. In the same way vanilla sandstone has several looks (chiseled, plain, etc.), Chisel 2 lets you choose different looks for many blocks. You have to craft the chisel tool and right-click it to open up a GUI (Graphic User Interface). Just insert the block you want to see variants of, then pull your choice out.

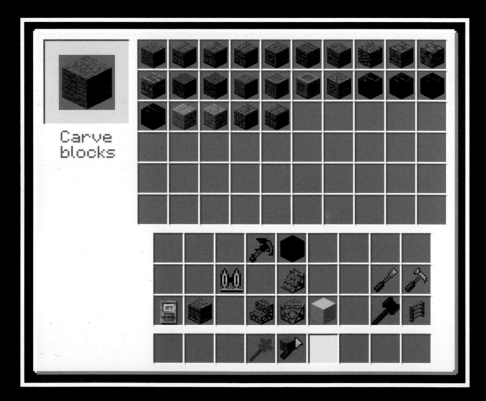

Place the Chisel 2 chisel and right-click to open the Chisel 2 GUI. Here you can drag a block and see the other styles Chisel 2 can transform it into.

This mod adds the Carpenter's Block, a kind of frame. You can add any texture from a second block, making the first block look just like the second. This gets interesting when there are more than one type of Carpenter's Block. Some will let you create angled blocks rather than square. There's the wedge slope, the stair, the ladder, the door, and more. Many of these Carpenter's Blocks can be turned to multiple positions and have several base textures to choose from.

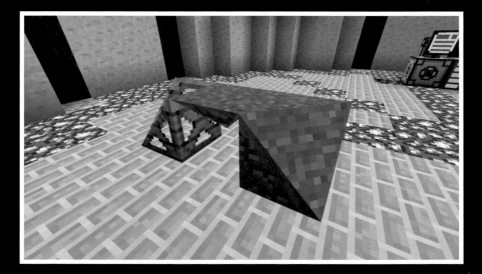

Carpenter's Blocks adds several blocks that have angles. You can cycle through how they are positioned using a Carpenter's Hammer, and apply a texture from another block to them. These angled blocks have been textured with a block of grass.

Use a Carpenter's Hammer to change the style of a Carpenter's Door, then right-click any block on the door to change its texture. Here, the lapis block was used to create the blue door.

Decocraft2

Authors: RazzleberryFox, taelnia, ProfMobius, lukitiki, Davexx100

Tired of fiddling around with stairs, fences, and slabs to make large clunky furniture? Struggle no more—add the mod Decocraft 2 and you'll have hundreds of objects to decorate your base, from grand pianos and laptops to Christmas trees, picnic baskets, canopy beds, and more.

Here are just a few of the kitchen-themed items from Decocraft.

BiblioCraft adds decorative objects to Minecraft as well, centered on a library theme. You can now replace all those oak bookshelves with spruce or any other wood, add chairs, desks, lamps, picture frames, and shelves.

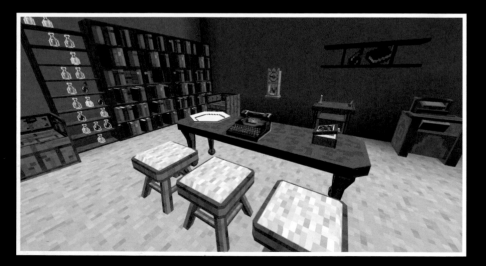

BiblioCraft adds lots of book and office-related items, like typewriters and shelves.

Pam's HarvestCraft

Author: MatrexsVigil

Pam's HarvestCraft adds tons of crops, bushes, fruit trees, and food, including vegetarian options, like soy milk and tofu. You don't have to limit yourself to steak, porkchops, and baked potatoes anymore. Pam's HarvestCraft has so many food options and recipes—there are even five types of donuts!

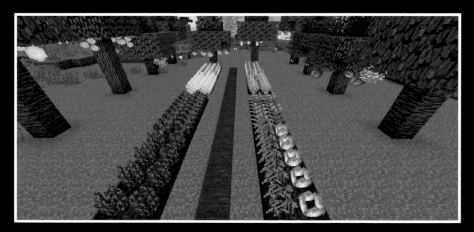

Create a garden of fruit and nut trees and really expand your home vegetable garden with Pam's HarvestCraft.

WorldEdit

Author: sk89q

WorldEdit is a mapmaking tool that lets you quickly create and destroy blocks in large numbers. You need to have Cheats enabled in your world in order for it to work. Although there is an Undo command, you can massively change your world with WorldEdit, so you do need to be careful of what you are doing. Things you can do include:

- Quickly create cubes, spheres, circles, and more out of any block.

- Copy, paste, and rotate a set of blocks.

- Use terraforming brushes to add, replace, and smooth blocks.

- Fix water problems and drain and fill pools.

- Create a forest.

- Save a copied area as a schematic to load into other worlds.

There is a little bit of a learning curve to WorldEdit, and you can find detailed information on this mod's capabilities at the World Edit wiki at wiki.sk89q.com/wiki/WorldEdit.

If you want an earth bridge to stretch out over your sci-fi dune landscape, WorldEdit can make it happen in minutes.

CHAPTER 8

PLAYING WITH MODPACKS

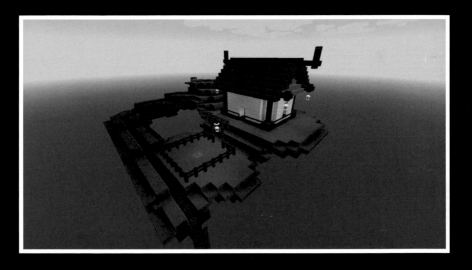

So once you've downloaded a modpack, what happens next? In the modpack launcher, just click the name of modpack you're starting, and a familiar Minecraft launcher will be started that has all the settings configured for you to play. (If you play with a really large pack of mods, you may want to increase your memory setting to 4GB, as long as your system has at least 8GB RAM.) You then create a new world in pretty much the same way you do in vanilla Minecraft. Find out if you are playing with the Biomes O' Plenty mod. If you are, you will have to set the World Type of your new world to Biomes O' Plenty. And for the few modpacks that include a specific map to play with, you'll have to select that world type in the Play screen.

Starting in a Modded World

When you arrive in your world, just follow vanilla procedures to get started. Punch wood, make a crafting table and some beginning tools, and gather a little food. You'll also want to prepare a temporary and safe home base. Mobs are generally much more dangerous in modded Minecraft because many mods add new, more powerful mobs. (You'll also have lots of ways to better protect yourself!) Keep a look out for the Natura mod's berry bushes and apple trees from Biomes O' Plenty. These are a great early food source.

The Natura berry bushes and the apple trees from Biomes O' Plenty mods are a great early food source, if you have them.

Most modpacks include NEI or a similar mod, Too Many Items (TMI), to help manage inventory. You can use NEI to look at what modpacks are installed and what items they provide. To see the mods installed, click **E** to open NEI, and then click the **Item Subsets** button to open different ways to explore the inventory. Click the **Mod** button to open up the list of mods, which you can scroll through. To see the objects and items added by a mod, type an at symbol (@) with the name of the mod, as in "@ Tinkers' Construct," in the NEI search box. The grid on the right will then show only the items from that modpack.

Use an inventory-management mod like NEI to see what mods are installed and what items they add.

One thing to be aware of: Modpacks sometimes change recipes for modded objects and items and vanilla items. For instance, in the Regrowth modpack, the crafting table is made with two wood slabs and two planks. And this is why modpacks include the NEI mod, because NEI helps you find all the recipes. The reason modpack authors do this is to tweak the rate at which you advance through learning and crafting new objects and technologies. They are balancing out the gameplay so you have to work a little more or explore a little more than normal.

You will also usually have JourneyMap or a similar mini-map mod installed. If you travel around, use the waypoint tool (press **D** in JourneyMap) to mark spots you'd like to come back to, like a ravine or a village, and your home base.

Once you've established yourself with some basic tools, a food source, and maybe a small animal farm, your next goal is usually to start amassing resources, like metals. If Tinkers' Construct mod is included, you'll want to create the four Tinkers' Construct blocks for crafting tools:

- **A Stencil Table:** To make stencils for tool parts.

- **A Stencil Chest:** To store these next to the part table.

- **The Parts Table:** Where you construct tool and weapon parts using the stencils and a permitted material. Place the Stencil Chest next to this to access the chests inventory.

- **The Tool Forge:** Where you combine two or more parts to create the final weapon or tool.

From left to right, the four Tinkers' Construct blocks you need to craft tools and weapons: Stencil Table, Stencil Chest, Parts Table, and Tool Forge.

The Tool Forge is the advanced version of the Tool Station, which you will usually create first, because it is cheaper to create. However, it doesn't include some of the advanced tools. When you have enough iron to spare, create the Tool Forge, so you can create a hammer. The hammer will mine out 3x3 tunnels. This single tool changes mining from being a real time-sink to great fun. And an excavator does the same for dirt and sand. And if you don't already have them, make the Tinkers' Construct guidebooks, Materials and You, Volumes 1 and 2, and Might Smelting, to help you with materials choices. At the beginning, before you have many resources, you can make tools with cobble—these are cheap to repair. Once you are able to make or gather obsidian, try to make your tools out of alumite—this alloy you create with the smeltery will let you mine the two top metal ores in the Nether: cobalt and ardite.

Early on, explore to find the villages in your area. If your modpack includes Tinkers' Construct, a village can spawn with a small smeltery ready for you to start using. I'll often look for a village right at the start, to help me get started with some resources. If you have a walled village, like those that the Witchery mod adds, it is usually pretty easy to secure the village walls and start playing with relatively little danger.

Something else to watch out for when starting to play mods is multiblock structures. These are structures built out of many blocks, like Tinkers' Construct smelteries. These multiblock structures don't become activated until they are built properly. Many mods that have multiblock structures include in-game books of instructions that appear when you spawn for the first time. If you are ever stuck, and you haven't found a book about the mod in your inventory or in NEI, a great place to start looking for information is the FTB wiki, at ftbwiki.org.

If the Witchery mod is installed in your modpack, a walled village is a great place to make your first base. Just close up the village entrances and light the village to help secure it.

Starting in an HQM World

An HQM modpack includes the mod Hardcore Questing Mode. With this, the modpack author has set up quests for you to follow, and you'll typically spawn with a quest book that you use to figure out your next task. In these worlds, follow the first quests—they will set you up with what you initially need to survive. Also note the word "Hardcore." In Minecraft, this means you have one life to live in the world—once you die, it's all over. However, most HQM modpacks give you several lives and opportunities along the way to earn more.

- -

One great way to start off with a specific modpack is to play along with a YouTuber that you like. Many Minecraft YouTubers have Let's Play series based on a modpack. You can see what they are up to, follow along, get inspired, copy, and learn. I'd recommend looking at direwolf20's modded, single-player Let's Play Season 7 series, using his own modpack called Direwolf20. You can download this modpack with the Curse launcher. Every ten episodes or so, direwolf20 posts links with the YouTube episode so you can download and play with his current world. Opening his world in your modded launcher means that you can see exactly how he is putting everything together. For an entertaining look at how creative you can get with a modpack, take a look at ethoslab's Etho's Modded Minecraft series.

direwolf20's Let's Play single-player YouTube series is a great way to follow along and play with an experienced modded Minecraft player. Here, direwolf20 contends with giant lookalikes in the Twilight Forest, using a pink slime crossbow.

The Agrarian Skies 1

Author: jadedcat

Because mods and modpacks can be very overwhelming—adding thousands of items, new types of gameplay, new interfaces for new machines, and more, I highly recommend starting out with one specific modpack: Agrarian Skies 1 (AS1). It is one of the most popular—if not the most popular—modpacks available.

The premise of Agrarian Skies 1 is that the world has been almost completely destroyed by monsters. A group of godlike mages have chosen you to try and rebuild the world starting from almost nothing on a tiny island. While the mages will help you, they will also ask for things in return. As it happens, they ask for a lot of things in return.

Agrarian Skies 1 is a great modpack to start with for several reasons. First, it has a fun storyline and includes the HQM questing system. The questing system gives you challenges to complete and rewards when you complete them, which will give you incentive for following all the quests.

Second, the pack is simply a great introduction to playing mods—it includes a number of the most popular and helps you start to find your way through them.

Third, Agrarian Skies 1 is a modded skyblock map. A skyblock map is an empty world with a little block of Minecraft land floating by itself in the sky (see the chapter opening image). If you fall off the edge, you will die in the Void. On the bright side, it is much easier to control hostile mobs spawning.

And finally, because the Agrarian Skies 1 modpack is so popular, it is fairly easy to find help and ideas on gameplay if you get stuck. Minecrafters have compiled lists of tips for Agrarian Skies 1, and many people have played it.

Note: While AS1 is based on Minecraft 1.6.4, the modpacks and skyblock setting prevent the pack from seeming out of date, especially if you are new to mods. There is also a new Agrarian Skies modpack, Agrarian Skies 2. At the time of writing, it is currently in beta, and is being updated fairly often, so I'll recommend starting with AS1. Many of the same concepts of the first Agrarian Skies apply to the second.

A few forums to look at for help are the AS1 tips and tricks lists on reddit.com and at Curse's FTB forum. However, you may find some spoilers here on gameplay elements that would otherwise surprise you.

- reddit.com/r/feedthebeast/comments/231p8t/ agrskies_agrarian_skies_tips_and_tricks/
- forum.feed-the-beast.com/threads/ spoiler-alert-agrarian-skies-hints-tips-secrets.44516/

Starting Agrarian Skies 1

1. Use the FTB launcher to download and install Agrarian Skies 1. Before starting the modpack, you'll also need to install the special map that comes with it. In the FTB launcher, click **Maps & Textures**. Press the **Maps** button to open the Maps screen. In the list of maps on the left, click **Agrarian Skies Default Map (v.1)** and then click **Install Map** to install the map.

2. In the FTB launcher, with Agrarian Skies 1 selected in the list of modpacks, click **Launch** to start the game. Click **Singleplayer** when the Minecraft screen opens. In the Select World Screen, select **Home Sweet Home T** and click **Play Selected World**. You'll arrive inside a single room house floating in the sky on some clay blocks. There are often update announcements from mod authors on the opening screen. You can ignore these, as your FTB launcher will update the modpack when necessary.

You start inside a tiny house on a skyblock in Agrarian Skies facing a chest.

3. In your inventory is a thin brown book called the quest book. This is what guides you through the mods. Right-click the quest book to open it, and read or play the introduction. When you're done with the introduction, click **Click Here** to start.

4. The quest book opens to show you the list of quest areas (there are multiple quests in each area). You'll see the number of lives you have left in the top right. This is a Hardcore map, meaning you only have a limited number of lives to play the map. However, quests along the way will help you gather more lives, and if you make it past the first week, you should be fine. The "Party" heading only applies if you are playing in a multiplayer setting, so you can ignore that. And under the Quests heading, you'll see your progress.

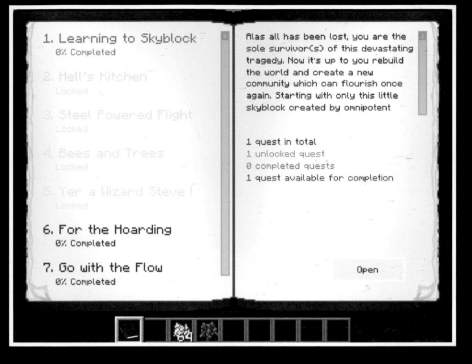

The quest book contents page lists the quest areas and shows your progress.

5. Open the chest in your house and notice there is no food. Not a scrap. You're going to have to be very careful to avoid hunger-inducing tasks (like jumping up blocks) until you get your food situation sorted out. You are going to have to grow oak trees and eat apples until you figure something else out. Luckily there is a fair amount of bonemeal you can use to get your trees started. (Also, take a look under your single block of dirt.)

6. You can get started on quests right away, as they help you survive the first few days. Select **1. Learning to Skyblock**, and on the right page, read the introduction to this area. Then, click **Open** to open the quest list. The quests appear as hexagonal buttons. They flash when they are ready to be played.

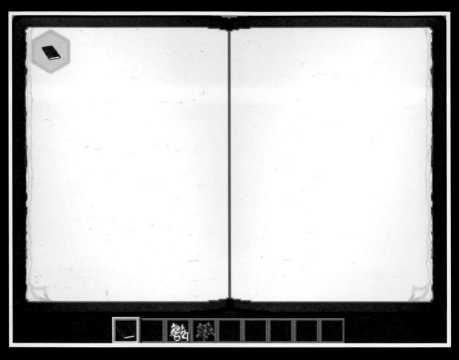

Each quest has a hexagonal button.

7. At first there is only one quest under Learning to Skyblock, but more will appear as you go on. Click the **Using the Book** quest icon to open the quest page and read your instructions. On the right page, you'll see what you have to provide or do in order to complete the quest. On the left is a description of the quest, followed by a list of the quest goals (there may be more than one), and a list of the rewards you will get for completing the quest. Sometimes you will have to choose between different options for your reward.

8. For the first quest, you must craft one block of planks, so you'll want to grow an oak tree, punch it down, and make a block of oak planks.

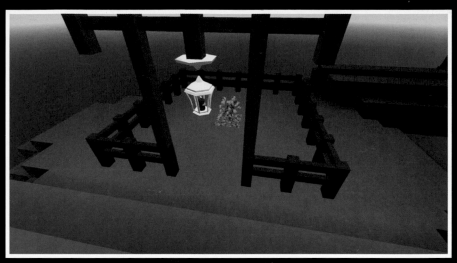

Plant your oak on the block of dirt outside.

9. Open the quest book again to your quest page. On the right, you'll see that you've completed the task. On the left, the **Claim Reward** button has activated, so click that to get your rewards.

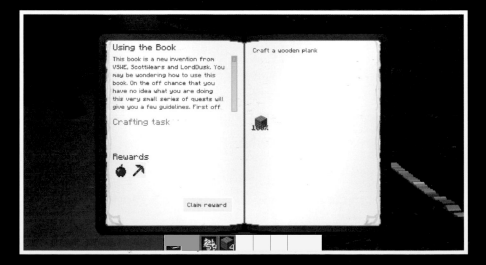

On the left page, click **Claim Reward** once you've finished the task.

10. Right-click a page to return to the previous page in the quest book. This takes you to the list of quests for Learning to Skyblock. You'll see that the icon for your completed quest is no longer flashing and two more quests have been unlocked. (If you ever see that a completed quest is still flashing and purple, this is because you can still claim a reward for it.)

11. After the first task, the quest book shows you other ways to complete tasks for the quest book. You can simply follow the quest book from here on out. Once you've resolved your food situation, you can start taking breaks from the quest book to improve your base or spend extra time on one mod or set of machines as you like.

Here are a few additional tips to help you manage your first week or so:

- If, for some reason, your first oak tree doesn't give you saplings, don't despair. You can submit items crafted with another wood type for quests until you get more oak seeds with later activities.

- When you set up the quest delivery system, right-click with the hopper to a side of the QDS block. You must use a pick to remove the hopper.

- Build a tree farm of at least 9 trees or more.

- Cooked silkworm is a decent food source.

- You can cook food in a pan without a furnace.

- If you are given the option of a slime sapling for a reward (or a slime bucket), choose it over anything else. Slime is hard to come by.

- When given a choice between a reward bag and another item, look in NEI to see how difficult it would be to make or get that item. You'll often find that the reward item is relatively easy to get, so you can feel good about taking that reward bag. Some reward bags have great stuff in them, others, not so much.

- Mobs don't spawn on bottom slabs (the slab that aligns with the bottom of a regular block). You can conserve wood and stop mobs from spawning by building out your base on half slabs.

- Make charcoal for torches.

- Try to gather and always keep several saplings of each type.

- Don't use up all the bonemeal you start out with; you will need some to make porcelain clay.

- Because there's nowhere for mobs to spawn, they'll spawn quickly wherever they can. This means you can build a simple mob farm of just an enclosed room some 20 blocks away from your base. Leave just a half-block-high space where the mob's feet will be so you can kill them and collect their drops.

To fish in the tiny pool, stand right in one corner, and look straight up to cast the line. The line will usually come down right into the pool and start bobbing. If it doesn't, try again.

You can also find loads of YouTube series on playing Agrarian Skies 1. Popular Minecraft YouTubers that have AS1 series include Generikb, direwolf20, Hypnotizd, and YOGSCAST.

CHAPTER 9

STARTING FTB INFINITY EVOLVED

FTB Infinity Evolved could be called the Cadillac of modpacks—or the kitchen sink of mod packs! It has the latest mods for magic, tech, exploration, and fun, all tweaked by the FTB team to work well together. It is also a bit of a monster, meaning it has LOTS of mods. You will need to have enough computer memory to assign 2GB or more to running it. It is not an HQM modpack, so you won't have any guidance in the game for playing. Here are steps to installing and starting your world with this modpack.

1. Download and install the Curse launcher at http://beta. cursevoice.com/games/minecraft.

2. In the Curse launcher, click **Browse FTB Modpacks**.

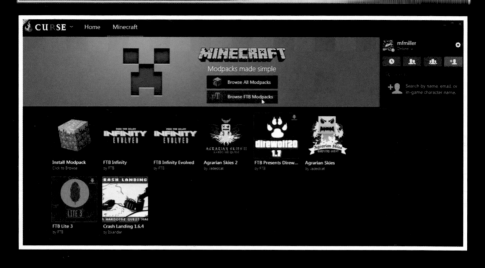

3. Locate FTB Infinity Evolved in the list that displays.

4. Click the **Install** button on the FTB Infinity Evolved icon to install the modpack. The Curse launcher will display the installation progress.

5. Once the modpack is installed, make sure you have enough RAM (computer memory) allocated. At the top right of the Curse launcher, click the gear icon and click **Settings** on the pull-down menu.

6. In the Curse Settings screen, select Minecraft on the left panel to open the Minecraft settings.

7. In the Java Settings section, make sure that the memory allocation amount is set to at least 2GB (on the far right of the slider here, it is set at 3GB). You can drag the circle on the slider to a new position. I set mine to 4GB.

8. Click **Save** to save your settings to return to the Curse launcher.

9. Now that the modpack is installed and your memory settings are set, mouse over the FTB Infinity Evolved Icon on the launcher. The icon will change to include an orange Play button. Click the **Play** button.

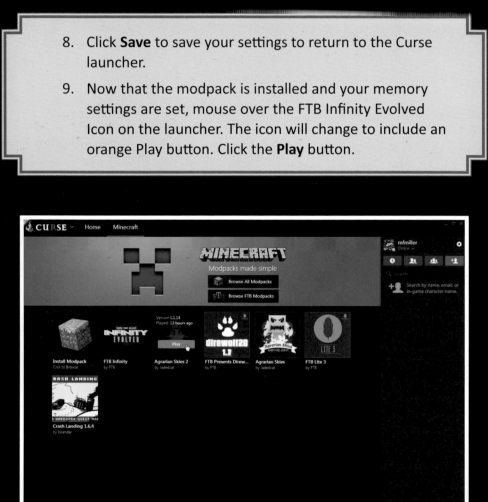

10. The Curse launcher will then open up the Minecraft launcher, already configured to work with the modpack. Click **Start** in the Minecraft launcher.

Minecraft Launcher 1.6.48

Update Notes | Launcher Log | Profile Editor

Minecraft News

Powered by Tumblr

Minecraft Realms survey

Update: Thanks everyone who participated! We have now closed the survey

~~Hello builders!~~

~~We're curious on what you know about various servers and how much you know about Realms. If we could have a minute or three of your time answering some questions, that would be great. Your answers will be super helpful for us to continue exploring new ideas and developing our services. Here's the link:~~

Thank you! <3

Minecraft 1.8.8

We have released Minecraft version 1.8.8 to fix some security issues and improved

Official links:

Minecraft.net
Minecraft Realms
Minecraft on Facebook
Merchandise

Bug tracker
Account Support

Mojang on Twitter
Support on Twitter

Try our other games!

Community

Profile: FTB Infinity ▼

New Profile | Edit Profile

Play

Welcome, **cappymiller**
Ready to play Minecraft forge-10.13.4.1448

Switch User

11. Next, the mod-loading screen will open, showing the progress in loading all of the mods.

12. Once the mods are loaded, the FTB Infinity Evolved start screen will open. Click **Singleplayer**.

13. The Select World screen will open. Click **Create New World**.

Select World

Play Selected World   Create New World
Rename   Delete   Re-Create   Cancel

14. If you've never played the modpack before, the Biomes O' Plenty splash screen opens to advise you on how to start a Biomes O' Plenty world. We'll do that now. Click **OK** to proceed.

Biomes O' Plenty uses a custom worldtype for its biomes. It may be enabled by clicking the 'World Type' button under 'More World Options' until it displays 'Biomes O' Plenty'.

The worldtype can be used on servers by changing the 'level-type' in server.properties to 'BIOMESOP' (without quotes).

This message will only display once.

OK

15. In the Create New World screen that opens, click **More World Options**.

16. In the World Options screen, click the **World Type: Default** button several times to cycle through the World Type options. Stop when you see **World Type: Biomes O' Plenty**.

17. If you like, add a seed in the Seed for the World
    Generator text box. This can be any string of
    characters, and it is used to create your world. Defining
    a seed means you can easily share it with others. If your
    seed generates a great world, your friends may want to
    use the same seed for their world. Here, I've typed in "a
    nest of chickens" for the seed. Let's see what that gets
    us. Click **Done** to return to the first Create New World
    screen.

18. Now type in a name for your world (I've used the seed for the name—"a nest of chickens"—which will help me remember the seed). Click **Create New World** to begin your game!

Create New World

World Name

a nest of chickens_

Will be saved in: a nest of chickens

Game Mode Survival

Search for resources, crafting, gain
levels, health and hunger

More World Options...

Create New World   Cancel

19. Congratulations! You've made it to your modded world! And, with my seed, I've landed in a swamp, with a couple of books in my hand! The books are guides to Tinkers' Construct mod, so I will hold on to them.

Playing On

Just like in vanilla Minecraft, my first goals in this FTB modpack (and any modpack, really) are tools, weapons, shelter, and food. There are willow trees in the swamp, and these are just as good as oak for making a crafting table and wooden tools. They're also one of my favorite trees, with a nice grayish-green color. Time to punch wood and craft a wood axe, shovel, pick, and sword.

Now, for a look about. This spawn looks pretty good because we are close to a magical forest, which will help later with playing some of the magical mods.

You can tell this is a Magical Forest Biome because of the magical, blue-leafed Silverwood tree.

There should be plenty of food around, beyond the meat you can get from cows, chickens, sheep, and pigs. I should be able to find berries from Natura berry bushes, as well as fruit trees, plants, and "gardens" added by the mod Pam's HarvestCraft. Breaking these gardens will give you plant items, many of which you can eat. There's a Berry Garden, Desert Garden, Gourd Garden, Grass Garden, Ground Garden, Herb Garden, Leafy Garden, Mushroom Garden, Stalk Garden, Textile Garden, Tropical Garden, and Water Garden.

Look out for Pam's HarvestCraft gardens, like this Stalk Garden. You can break it to get eggplants, beans, bell peppers, and more. You can eat these vegetables or place them in a crafting grid to make seeds to grow your own vegetables. You can also search in NEI for the recipes that use them to make special foods, like Eggplant Parm.

Here's a cow with a hat. The Hats mod adds random and strange hats to mobs. You have to kill the mob to get its hat. Once you do, press H to open the Hat settings screen and select the hat you want to wear.

What I like to do first is find a village. Villages are one of my favorite things in large modpacks because different mods add new buildings, resources, walls, and villager traders. Plus, they look really cool. Villages also spawn more frequently in the Infinity modpacks so it doesn't take as long to find a village. So now that I have my first tools, I'm going to explore and gather food as I go. I especially want to kill sheep for wool to make a bed so I'll be able to sleep to avoid the monsters for now.

You will find hobgoblins as you explore. They are a neutral mob to players so they won't attack you unless you attack them first.

I find a village not too far from spawn, at X=677, Z=737. The Witchery mod adds sentry guards who will attack any mobs. However, they aren't foolproof. Until I secure the village by improving walls and lighting, I will need to fall asleep at sunset to stop the mob. But I am home free! It's time to start playing around with mods. You'll want to first explore Tinkers' Construct for creating better weapons and tools and start mining for the best ores. Once you have better weapons, the mods you play with are up to you. I usually start with the tech mods. I concentrate on mining and improving my resource-gathering with the machines from the Thermal Expansion and MineFactory Reloaded mods. Once I have tons of resources (metals, gems, and more) pouring in, I build advanced storage and crafting with Applied Energistics. However, an equally valid way to start is with the magical mods. These can have you up and running with super resources and gear quickly, too, and I may try this on my next modded world!

I found a nice big village, with lots of the buildings added by mods: an Apiarist's house with goodies to get started playing with bees, an Agricraft greenhouse, a Tinkers' house, a smeltery, and more.

To explore the FTB Infinity Evolved mods further, visit the FTB wikis, which cover the mods the FTB team uses in their modpacks. These are my go-to sources, along with using Google for specific questions. There's the unofficial FTB wiki, at ftbwiki.org, and the official FTB wiki, at ftb.gamepedia.com. There are also some helpful Getting Started tutorials at ftb.gamepedia.com/Getting_Started_(Main). You can find links to these sites and more at my website, meganfmiller.com. See you there!

APPENDIX

To start working with mods individually, you will need to have intermediate to advanced computer skills, including:

a) Knowing what zipped files are and how to work with them.

b) Knowing how to navigate your file system.

c) Knowing how to find a mod online, and making sure you have read all the requirements for a mod and instructions for installing it.

d) Understanding that some mods may conflict with each other, especially mods that are modifying the same types of activities in Minecraft (for example, two mods that modify Minecraft villagers).

e) Making backups of your Minecraft worlds.

f) Being able to troubleshoot crashes and incompatibilities using online resources, such as the Minecraft wiki, the Minecraft Forum, relevant mod forums, and Reddit forums.

Installing a Mod with MultiMC 5

1. To install MultiMC, go to the MultiMC website at https://multimc.org and download the application that is right for your platform (Windows, Mac, or Linux). A zipped folder will download.

2. Once the download is finished, open the zipped folder and drag the folder that is inside—labeled MultiMC— to your hard drive. Since there isn't a regular installer

for the program, you'll need to remember where you drag this folder to. The location that you drag it to will be the location where the program runs from

3. Then, to run the MultiMC program, open the MultiMC folder and double-click the MultiMC.exe file.

4. Next, you will want to change your settings in MultiMC. First, click the **Accounts** button at the top right, and select **Manage Accounts**. This opens up the Settings dialog box to the Accounts tab. (You can also click the **Change Settings** button in the top menu bar.)

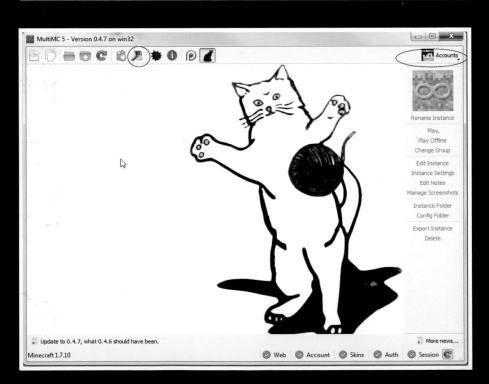

To change settings, click the **Change Settings** button in the menu bar (circled in red). You can also click **Accounts** in the top right and then select **Manage Accounts**.

5. In the Accounts tab, add your Minecraft profile (your email/username and password).

6. In the Java tab, change the default maximum memory specified in the Maximum memory allocation box. Mods, and especially modpacks, use quite a bit more computer memory than vanilla Minecraft. You shouldn't set Maximum memory allocation to more than half of your computer memory and, if possible, set this to 1GB (1024 MB) or 2 GB (2048 MB).

Mods take up more memory so you will usually want to change the maximum memory allocation in the Java tab. You can use the arrows in the spin box to change the memory allocation.

7. In the Minecraft window, you can change the size of the window that the Minecraft game starts in. If you want the game to run full screen, select the **Start Minecraft maximized** check button.
8. Close the Settings dialog box.
9. Create a new instance (essentially a copy of the Minecraft game that you will use chosen mods with) by clicking the **New Instance** button on the left of the top menu bar.
10. In the **New Instance** dialog box, name your instance. Here, I've called this instance "First."

In the New Instance dialog box, you can name your instance, create or select a group to put it in, and specify which version of Minecraft you are using. Instead of working with vanilla Minecraft, you can choose to use a downloaded modpack instead.

11. Under **Vanilla Minecraft**, click the **...** button and then select **1.7.10** as the version of Minecraft to use and click **OK**. (Minecraft 1.7.10 currently has the most number of mods available for it.)
12. Click **OK** to close the New Instance dialog box. The program will update to download the right files for the Minecraft version you selected.
13. Right-click the icon for the instance, and select **Edit Instance**.
14. In the Edit Instance dialog box, click the **Install Forge** button. This will open up a window to confirm which version of Forge to install. Keep the recommended Forge version (this will have a star next to it) and click **OK**.

Version	Branch
Forge 10.13.4.1481	1.7.10
Forge 10.13.4.1472	1.7.10
Forge 10.13.4.1470	1.7.10
Forge 10.13.4.1469	1.7.10
Forge 10.13.4.1456	1.7.10
Forge 10.13.4.1452	1.7.10
Forge 10.13.4.1451	1.7.10
Forge 10.13.4.1448	1.7.10
Forge 10.13.4.1447	1.7.10
Forge 10.13.4.1445	1.7.10
Forge 10.13.3.1428	1.7.10
Forge 10.13.3.1424	1.7.10
Forge 10.13.3.1422	1.7.10
Forge 10.13.3.1420	1.7.10
Forge 10.13.3.1408	1.7.10

Refresh   OK   Cancel

In the Select Forge version dialog box, the version of Forge that is recommended for you to use with the Minecraft version you selected will have a yellow star beside it.

15. Click **Close** to close the Edit Instance dialog box.
16. Open your central mods folder by clicking the blue folder with a gold star icon in the menu bar. This folder is a handy place to keep your downloaded mods, as MultiMC will look here first when you later add mods to an instance.
17. Next, download the mods you want to use to your central mods folder you opened in the previous step. WARNING: These downloaded mods will have to be compatible with the version of Forge and Minecraft you are using. Some mods also require you to install other mods (requirements). You will need to make sure to download and install any requirements. Two places to find mods are
    a. Curse: curse.com/mc-mods/minecraft
    b. The Minecraft Forum: minecraftforum.net/
18. I've downloaded the mod Not Enough Items and a required file, CodeChickenCore, from the mod author's site at chickenbones.net.
19. Once you have downloaded the mod you want, you'll need to add it to your instance. With your instance selected in the main MultiMC panel, click **Edit Instance** in the right panel.
20. Click the **Install Mods** button on the right. You can also click the **Loader Mods** tab on the left.
21. In the Loader mods tab, click the **Add** button on the right. This will open up your central MultiMC mods folder.
22. Select the mod or mods you want to add and click **Open**.
23. Click **Close** to close the Edit Instance dialog box.
24. You are now ready to play Minecraft with the mod(s) you have just added. Double-click the instance in the main panel to start your modded Minecraft game. If a

console window opens, you can minimize it or move this out of the way of your game window.
25. When your Minecraft game start window opens, you can start the game. To play your modded game at a later date, you'll have to again open the MultiMC launcher and double-click your instance.

Your starting window will show what version of Minecraft you are using along with the version of Forge and the number of mods that are loaded and active. You can also click the Mods button to see a list of active mods.

Tip: If you are going to use a lot of different instances, you can create groups to organize your instances into. You can select or create a group when you first create an instance or by right-clicking an instance and selecting **Change Group** in the dropdown menu.